Taste and Tales of Massachusetts

Written and Edited by
P. Ann Pieroway

Cover and Illustrations by
Louise Minks, Massachusetts Artist

Designed by
Catherine Cornwell

To Kathy,
Bon Appetit!
Ann Pieroway

Bass Pond
PRESS

Springfield, MA

Taste and Tales of Massachusetts
Published by Bass Pond Press
Springfield, Massachusetts
www.basspondpress.com

P.O. Box 6
East Longmeadow, MA 01028

Millworks Studio at the Montague Mill
Montague Center, MA 01351

Designed by Catherine Cornwell

Library of Congress Cataloging-in-Publication Data
Pieroway, P. Ann
Taste and Tales of Massachusetts, A Collection... / P. Ann Pieroway
Cover and Illustrations by Louise Minks
ISBN 0-9755794-0-1

Printed in Massachusetts
First Printing: 2004
5,000 copies

Cover Painting by Louise Minks
Hart Haven, Martha's Vineyard

Introduction

Writing this cookbook brings together two of my favorite hobbies — cooking and history. Massachusetts is the home of baked beans, Boston cream pie and cranberries, but before that, there were the Native Americans and early English Puritan settlers known to us as Pilgrims. One of America's most cherished holidays is Thanksgiving, which has been attributed to a feast that occurred in Massachusetts in 1621.

From Boston to the Berkshires, to the islands of Nantucket and Martha's Vineyard, come a myriad of taste and three centuries of history. These marvelous foods are a result of the many nationalities, past and present, that call Massachusetts home. These include the English, Irish, Portuguese, Italians, Polish, French, Africans, Russians and other Eastern Europeans, and in more recent years, Hispanics and Asians. These many cultures are responsible for the variety of foods that are found across the Commonwealth.

I hope you enjoy the *Taste and Tales of Massachusetts* as much as I have taken pleasure in writing it.

— P. Ann Pieroway

Dedication

This book is dedicated to my mother, ***Phoebe E. Pieroway***, who instilled in me a love of cooking at an early age; and to my brother and late father who ate what I made when I was young, and never—well, hardly ever—complained.

Special thanks go to family and friends who have encouraged me to write this book for many years, and to Louise Minks and Cathy Cornwell who believed that I could do it. The three of us make a great team.

About the Artist

Louise Minks lives in rural Western Massachusetts. Her working studio gallery, Millworks Studio, is located at the Montague Mill in Montague Center. She is in galleries in Massachusetts, Vermont and New Mexico, and in many private collections. Louise can be contacted via her website is www.artistseverywhere.net.

A portion of the profits from the *Taste and Tales of Massachusetts* will be dedicated to selected projects that will benefit the libraries, gardens and parks of Massachusetts.

Table of Contents

*All temperatures in degrees Fahrenheit. For our friends from overseas, metric conversions are provided in the back of the book.

Appetizers and Beverages

Rockport

Cows on the Common

The Boston Common, one of the oldest public parks in the country, was owned originally by William Blackstone and used primarily as a pasture. Upon becoming a public park, it became illegal to graze cows on the Common. Today, the Common is the heart of Boston. In the winter there is skating on Frog Pond; and in the warmer months, visitors and residents alike are seen performing Tai Chi or walking their pets. The Common hosts many parties throughout the year, from First Night in January to the annual lighting of the Christmas trees. The first football game in America was played on the Boston Common around 1860.

I remember as a teenager walking through the Common, which was resplendent with the symbols of Christmas – from Yule logs to reindeer.

Raspberry Brie en Croûte

1 (7-inch) round loaf of rye or sourdough bread
1 (5-inch) round Brie cheese
½ cup seedless raspberry jam
¼ cup chopped almonds

1. Preheat oven to 325°.
2. Slice off ½ inch from top of bread using a serrated knife. Reserve top of bread.
3. Place Brie cheese on top of bread; trace around outer edge of cheese with knife. Using traced mark as a guide, carefully cut bread vertically 2 inches deep (do not cut through bread); remove bread.
4. Remove white rind from top of Brie with serrated knife. Place Brie cheese in cavity.
5. Spread top with jam and sprinkle with sliced almonds.
6. Bake for 15 to 20 minutes or just until soft.
7. Serve immediately with fresh fruit slices, crackers, chips or cubed bread.

Why is Rockport a Dry Town?

For the past 150 years, visitors and residents of the seaside village of Rockport have been unable to purchase a drop of alcohol within the town's boundaries. It all started on July 8, 1856 when a group of about 75 women marched to town dressed in matching outfits of calico dresses, gingham aprons, bonnets and shawls. Considering the time of year, the women were dressed rather warmly.

According to the Sandy Bay Historical Society, the women dressed in this fashion to hide the hatchets that they were carrying. It took the women about six hours, but when they went home, there was not a drop of liquor to be found in Rockport, and it has remained that way ever since. Why did the women take to the streets? They were tired of their husbands drinking the monies they earned and felt that by getting rid of the problem (the liquor), the spouses would have naught on which to spend their hard earned money.

Hot Crabmeat Hors d'oeuvres

12 ounces crabmeat, drain well
2 (8-ounce) packages cream cheese
2 tablespoons mayonnaise
2 teaspoons Worcestershire sauce
2 teaspoons lemon juice
Season to taste

1. Preheat oven to 350°.
2. Mix all ingredients together and put in an ovenproof casserole dish.
3. Bake until hot and bubbly for about 30 minutes.
4. Serve with crackers, carrots and celery sticks or a ripple-type chip.

Blue Hills of Massachusetts

The name Massachusetts comes from the Algonquin Indian words that mean "near the great mountain." It is felt that this references an area south of Milton known as the Blue Hills.

Massachusetts is one of four states in the Union to be known as a commonwealth (others include Kentucky, Pennsylvania and Virginia). A commonwealth is a body of people in a politically organized community that is independent or semi-independent, and in which the government functions by the common consent of the people. (Encarta® Encyclopedia 2000)

Portobello Mushrooms

6 (4-inch) portobello mushrooms
Boursin cheese
Balsamic vinaigrette
Salt and pepper to taste
1 tablespoon garlic, minced

1. Preheat 400°.
2. Remove stems, wash and dry mushrooms. Place mushrooms bottom down in large baking dish.
3. Combine vinaigrette, salt, pepper and garlic. Pour over mushrooms. Cover and marinate for 8 to 12 hours.
4. Place mushrooms on baking sheet and bake in oven for 8 to 10 minutes, until center is soft.
5. Remove from oven and spread Boursin cheese on top. Return to oven and bake until bubbly and lightly golden; remove from oven.
6. Cut mushrooms into quarters and serve with toothpicks. Serve immediately.

Sea Scallops in Mushrooms Caps

2 dozen large mushrooms
Salt and pepper
2 dozen sea scallops
6 slices bacon
Chopped parsley (optional)

1. Preheat broiler, using maximum setting.
2. Wash mushrooms and pat dry with paper toweling. Remove stems and place mushrooms caps upside down on a cookie sheet.
3. Season mushrooms with salt and pepper and place a sea scallop on each mushroom. Lay ¼ slice bacon over each mushroom.
4. Broil about two inches from heat for 8 to 10 minutes, depending on size of mushrooms. Garnish with chopped parsley before serving, if desired.

Yield: 24 stuffed mushroom caps

Lobster Canapés

3 tablespoons butter
1½ cups freshly grated Parmesan cheese
1 egg yolk
3 tablespoons dry sherry
⅛ teaspoon cayenne pepper
½ teaspoon Worcestershire sauce
1½ cups cooked lobster meat, finely chopped
48 toasted bread rounds, 1½ to 2-inch

1. Preheat oven to 425°.
2. Cream the butter and cheese together. Stir in egg yolk, sherry, cayenne and Worcestershire sauce. Add lobster and mix well.
3. Place a spoonful of the lobster mixture on each toast round. Place on a baking sheet and bake for 5 minutes.

Yield: 4 dozen

Famous Firsts

So many firsts happened, and continue to happen, in Massachusetts. It only seems appropriate that they all began with the first Thanksgiving in 1621.

Academically, the firsts include:

- Harvard University, first American university (1636)
- Boston Latin School, first American public school (1635)

Other firsts in America include:

- Boston Commons, first public park (1634)
- Boston Public Library, first public library (1653)
- Arsenal at Springfield, first federal arsenal (1777)
- Boston News-Letter, first regularly issued newspaper, (1704)
- Mount Auburn Cemetery in Watertown and Cambridge, first landscaped cemetery (1831)

Oysters Falmouth

2 dozen oysters
4 tablespoons butter
1 teaspoon onion juice
1 teaspoon oregano
Freshly ground pepper to taste
Unseasoned breadcrumbs
4 slices proscuitto, cut in thin slices
¼ cup Parmesan cheese, freshly grated

1. Preheat oven to 350°.
2. Shuck oysters; leave on half-shell on a cookie sheet.
3. Melt butter with onion juice; add to oysters. Lightly top each oyster with breadcrumbs. Sprinkle with oregano and pepper.
4. Place slice of proscuitto on top and grate cheese on top.
5. Bake for 15 minutes and serve.

Mushrooms with Crabmeat Stuffing

30 large mushrooms
Butter
½ onion, minced
4 ounces butter
1 ounce white wine
1 teaspoon parsley flakes
¼ loaf bread (remove crust, grind bread coarse)
1 pound crabmeat, chopped coarse

Mornay Sauce:
4 ounces butter
4 ounces flour
4 cups milk
½ cup white wine
1½ cups Swiss cheese, shredded
1 teaspoon Worcestershire sauce
Salt and pepper to taste

1. Snap stems off mushrooms. Saute mushrooms in butter for 5 minutes. Cool and set aside.
2. Saute onion in butter and cool. Add wine, parsley flakes, bread crumbs and crabmeat to onions; mix well. Salt and pepper to taste.
3. Make a roux by melting 4 ounces of butter and combining with flour. Continue to stir with whisk until smooth. Bring milk to boil, then gradually add to roux. Whisk until it thickens.
4. Add the remaining ingredients; mix well. Strain sauce; let cool. Add a little sauce to filling (a couple of teaspoons). Fill mushrooms; cover with Mornay sauce.
5. Bake for 10 minutes at 450°.

Yield: 30 mushrooms

Broiled Scallops Nantucket

24 scallops
24 pineapple wedges
24 (4-inch) strips of bacon

1. Place a scallop and pineapple wedge at opposite ends of each bacon strip. Roll strip towards the center so scallop and pineapple are wrapped in bacon. Secure with toothpicks.
2. Broil until bacon is crisp, about 10 minutes, turning to brown all sides. Serve immediately.

More Massachusetts Firsts

Transportation firsts:

- Railroad built in Quincy (1826)
- Commercially-sold gas powered car by Duryea in Springfield (1892)
- Subway (now known as MBTA) opened in Boston (1898)
- Nuclear powered surface warship, USS Long Beach, commissioned in Quincy (1961)

Other firsts include: basketball in Springfield (1891), volleyball in Holyoke (1895), the computer in Cambridge (1928), the first e-mail message sent from Cambridge (1971), frozen foods created by Birds Eye Frosted Foods® (1930) and the first scenic road for touring the Mohawk Trail (1914). These are only a few of the more notable firsts. There are many more as Massachusetts continues to be on the leading edge of technology.

Shrimp Ball

8 ounces cream cheese
1 (4-ounce) can shrimp, small
1 teaspoon lemon juice
2 tablespoons horseradish, squeezed
½ cup chili sauce

1. Mix cream cheese, shrimp, lemon juice and two tablespoons of horseradish together and roll into a ball.
2. Mix the chili sauce and horseradish mixture together and pour over ball.
3. Serve with crackers.

Ipswich Steamed Clams with Broth

3 quarts soft shell clams (steamers)
½ cup boiling water
Butter, melted

1. Wash clams thoroughly. Place in a steamer, add the water and cover.
2. Steam for 5 to 10 minutes, or until clams open. Discard any clams that do not open.
3. Drain clams, reserving broth.
4. Serve with broth and melted butter in separate dishes.

Sausage and Cheddar Biscuits

1 pound sharp Cheddar cheese, shredded
1 pound bulk sausage
3 cups dry biscuit baking mix

1. Preheat oven to 400°.
2. In a large saucepan, heat together sausage and shredded cheese. Stir with wood spoon until cheese has melted.
3. Stir in biscuit mix until smooth. Cool. Chill for about 30 minutes.
4. Shape into small balls about the size of a quarter. Place on ungreased baking sheet.
5. Bake for 8 to 10 minutes. Remove; place on paper toweling to drain. Serve warm.

Yield: About 4 dozen

Cook's Note:
Biscuits may be frozen after baking. Reheat in a low oven.

Running of the Marathoners

The Boston Marathon is the oldest marathon in North America. In 1996, it celebrated its 100th year when 36,748 starters began the 26.2-mile run from Hopkinton over Heartbreak Hill to finish in Copley Square (35,810 finished). The race is run each April on Patriot's Day, a Massachusetts holiday celebrating the beginning battles of the American Revolution. One can't help but wonder what came first, the holiday or the marathon. Massachusetts also celebrates Evacuation Day (when the British left Boston) on St. Patrick's Day. Only in Massachusetts!

Swedish Meatballs

4 tablespoons butter
⅓ cup onion, minced
1 egg
½ cup milk
½ cup fresh bread crumbs
1¼ teaspoons salt
2 teaspoons sugar
Pinch allspice
Pinch nutmeg
1 pound ground chuck or top round
¼ pound pork, ground
3 tablespoons flour
1 teaspoon sugar
1¼ teaspoons pepper
1 cup water
¾ cup light cream

1. In two tablespoons of hot butter in large skillet, sauté onion until golden.
2. In a large mixing bowl, beat egg; add milk and bread crumbs. Let stand 5 minutes.
3. Add salt, sugar, allspice, nutmeg, meats and onion. Blend well with fork.
4. In same skillet, heat another two tablespoons butter. Shape into ½- to ¾- inch balls. Drop in skillet. Brown well on all sides. Remove to warm casserole.
5. Into fat left in skillet, stir flour, sugar, salt and pepper. Slowly add water, cream and stir until thickened.

Yield: About 5 dozen

Spinach-Cheese Puffs

1 large onion, pared and minced
¼ cup olive oil
1¼ pounds spinach leaves, cleaned, stems trimmed, and finely chopped
1 pound feta cheese, drained and finely crumbled
6 eggs, beaten
1 cup chicken or veal velouté
1 teaspoon white peppercorns, freshly ground
1 pound fillo pastry shells
1 pound melted butter

1. Preheat oven to 425º.
2. Sauté onion in olive oil until transparent; add spinach and let cool.
3. Add feta, stirring to evaporate water. Add eggs, velouté and peppercorns. Taste and adjust seasonings.
4. Brush 2 fillo sheets at a time with melted butter. (Keep remaining sheets covered.) Stack the 2 sheets and cut into 3-inch strips. Place 1 tablespoon of the filling at one end of each strip; fold like a flag.
5. Bake for 15 minutes or until puffed and golden.

Yields: 4 dozen

Cook's Note:
Velouté is a white sauce made with stock instead of milk.

Pineapple Cheese Spread

¼ cup crushed pineapple, drained
1 (3-ounce) package cream cheese, softened
1-2 teaspoons prepared horseradish

1. Combine pineapple, cream cheese and horseradish (add horseradish to taste).
2. Place spread in small serving bowl. Cover and chill overnight.
3. Serve with crackers.

Yield: ½ cup

Lighting the Way

Historically, Massachusetts was a seafaring state and to many degrees, it still is. Today instead of the massive fishing vessels that plied the waters around eastern Massachusetts, you have recreational boats of all sizes. To show boaters the way after dark or in the fog, there are many lighthouses dotting the coastline. Martha's Vineyard alone has five – West Chop, Gay Head, East Chop, Edgartown Harbor and Chappaquiddick. Then there is Cape Ann, Marblehead, Boston Harbor, Truro and oh, so many more.

Boston Light at the entrance of Boston Harbor was the first lighthouse built in North America (1716) and the last to be automated (1998). It was built on Little Brewster Island, also known as Beacon Island. To finance Boston Light, a tax of one penny per ton was charged on all vessels coming into or out of the harbor. Boston Light was destroyed in the Revolution and rebuilt in 1783.

Beer Cheese Spread

6 ounces cream cheese, softened
6 ounces Blue cheese, softened
12 ounces sharp white Cheddar cheese, grated
¼ cup green onions, minced
1 teaspoon paprika
½ teaspoon celery salt
½ teaspoon ground black pepper
½ teaspoon Tabasco® sauce
½ cup full-bodied ale

1. Combine all ingredients, except ale, in a food processor or blender. Mix or blend until everything is well-blended.
2. Slowly add beer while the processor or blender is running. Place in a crock or serving bowl and chill until firm.
3. Serve with crackers, pretzels, sliced apples or pears and even a hearty beer bread.

Yield: 1½ pounds

Three Arts Society

The third oldest theater in the nation, the Berkshire Playhouse, began its start as a casino. The opening night was held was on June 4, 1928. It was moved to its present location on Main Street in Stockbridge, after the members of the Three Arts Society purchased it for one dollar. A financier, Walter Clark; a sculptor, Daniel Chester French; a psychiatrist, Austen Fox Riggs; and a drama critic, Walter Eaton made up the Society. These men set about to change the casino into a legitimate theater. In 1967, the Berkshire Playhouse was renamed the Berkshire Theatre Festival. A few of the many great artists who have performed at the Stockbridge Playhouse include Katherine Hepburn, James Cagney, Jane Wyatt, Claude Rains, Lillian Gish and Montgomery Clift. The Playhouse is on the National Historic Register and a member of the National Trust.

Bacon Chive Dip

¾ pound bacon, uncooked
1¼ pounds cream cheese
¼ cup red onion, minced
1 cup sour cream
⅛ cup fresh parsley, chopped
½ teaspoon A-1® sauce
1 teaspoon garlic, minced
½ teaspoon Worcestershire sauce
⅛ cup fresh chives, chopped

1. Chop bacon in food processor. Then cook in a sauté pan until fully cooked, drain on paper toweling and cool.
2. Remove stems and chop parsley in food processor; reserve.
3. Mix all ingredients in bowl until smooth.
4. Store in airtight container in refrigerator until ready to serve.
5. Serve with chips, vegetables or crackers.

Source: Daniel Webster Inn
Sandwich

Anyone Need a Whip?

Westfield earned its nickname, "The Whip City", during the horse and buggy era that lasted from the mid-1800s into the early 20th century. During this time period, over 90 percent of the world's supply of horsewhips were made in Westfield. No one is really sure who started the industry or why it began in Westfield, but at its height, there were over 30 companies employing many hundreds of people making whips.

By 1892, the U.S. Whip Company produced 25,000 finished whips per day. The emergence of the horseless-carriage soon caused the demise of the once burgeoning industry. Today only one company, Westfield Whip, continues to make this unique product that gave a city its most unusual nickname.

Shrimp Dip

1 pint sour cream
1 package onion soup mix
3 tablespoons horseradish
¾ cup chili sauce
2 cans small shrimp
Few drops Tabasco® sauce

1. Mix all ingredients and mix well.
2. Serve with crackers or shrimp.

Yield: 2 cups

Mexican Dip

8 ounces cream cheese
1 (16-ounce) can refried beans
¼ cup black olives, sliced
¼ cup tomatoes, diced
¼ cup peppers, chopped (red, green or yellow)
1 (26-ounce) jar salsa
8 ounces Monterey Jack or Cheddar cheese

1. Preheat oven to 350º.
2. Layer cream cheese, refried beans, olives, tomatoes, peppers and salsa in a pie plate.
3. Sprinkle top with cheese.
4. Bake until cheese is melted and slightly browned. Allow to cool.
5. Reheat in microwave (tastes best when reheated).
6. Serve warm with tortilla chips.

Jezebel

1 (10-ounce) jar of pineapple or apricot preserves
1 (10-ounce) jar of apple jelly
2 tablespoons mustard powder
2-4 tablespoons horseradish
Large block cream cheese

1. Mix all ingredients together except cream cheese.
2. To serve, pour mixture over cream cheese on serving dish. Serve with crackers or sliced vegetables. Sauce can be stored in refrigerator for up to two weeks.

Silk Worms of Northampton

The Chinese might have fooled King James I, who desperately wanted to start a silk industry in England, by sending him mulberry trees that bear black fruit instead of white, but the founders of the silk industry in Northampton did not make the same mistake. It began in the 1830s and continued until the Great Depression of the mid-1930s. If you drive by the corner of Nonotuck and Corticelli streets, there stands a very old, very gnarled mulberry tree — a silent reminder of a once-thriving industry.

Vegetable Dip

2 cups sour cream
2 cups mayonnaise
½ teaspoon marjoram
½ teaspoon thyme
½ teaspoon oregano
¼ teaspoon salt
½ teaspoon curry
½ teaspoon parsley
1 small onion, grated
½ teaspoon lemon juice
1 teaspoon Worcestershire sauce
2 teaspoons crushed capers (optional)

1. Mix together and chill.
2. Serve with mushrooms, celery, broccoli, carrots, radishes, cherry tomatoes and cauliflower.

Yield: 2 cups

The Town of Seven Railroads

At the beginning of the 20th century, Palmer was known as the town of seven railroads. It was the hub of train activity for all of New England when 30 to 40 trains stopped daily at the Romanesque Depot. Designed by architect Henry Hobson Richardson with landscaping by Frederick Law Olmsted, the depot is now an antique store.

Hot Mushroom Turnovers

1 (8-ounce) package cream cheese, softened
1½ cups flour, all-purpose
½ cup butter, softened
3 tablespoons butter
½ pound mushrooms, minced
1 large onion, minced
¼ cup sour cream
1 teaspoon salt
¼ teaspoon dried thyme
2 tablespoons flour
1 egg, beaten

1. In a large bowl, beat cream cheese, flour and butter on medium speed until smooth; shape into ball. Wrap in a cellophane wrap and refrigerate for 1 hour.
2. In a skillet, melt butter and sauté onion and mushrooms until tender, stirring occasionally. Stir in sour cream, salt, thyme and flour; set aside.
3. On a floured surface, roll out half the dough ⅛-inch thick with floured rolling pin. With floured 2¾-inch round cookie cutter, cut out as many circles as possible. Repeat with other half of dough.
4. Preheat oven to 450º.
5. Onto one half of each dough piece, place a teaspoon of mushroom mixture. Brush edge of circle with beaten egg; fold dough over filling. With fork, firmly press edges together to seal; prick tops.
6. Place turnovers on ungreased cookie sheet; brush with remaining egg. Bake 12 to 14 minutes until golden brown.

Cook's Note:
These turnovers are wonderful frozen too. When finished with step 5, simply place in a sealed plastic bag and place in freezer. When ready to use, place on cookie sheet and bake.

Land Far Out to Sea

Native Americans gave Nantucket Island its name meaning "faraway island" or "land far out to sea." Since Nantucket is 30 miles from the mainland in Hyannis, it certainly lives up to its name.

In 1602, approximately 1,500 members of the Wampanoag Tribe inhabited the island when Captain Bartholomew Gosnold discovered it. Nantucket's history as an English settlement began about fifty years later when Thomas Mayhew sold his interests in the island for thirty pounds and two beaver hats.

Nantucket was considered the Whaling Capital of the World from 1800 to 1840. During its whaling days, it was the third largest city in Massachusetts, with a population of 10,000 (only Boston and Salem were larger). Nantucket is the only place in the United States with the same name for an island, county and town.

Cheddar Cheese Strips

½ pound sharp Cheddar cheese, shredded
6 slices bacon, cooked and crumbled
1 small package slivered almonds
2 teaspoons Worcestershire sauce
1 small onion, finely chopped
1 cup mayonnaise
Salt and pepper
1 loaf Arnold's® white bread

1. Preheat oven to 400°.
2. Mix together cheese, bacon, almonds, Worcestershire sauce, onion, mayonnaise, salt and pepper.
3. Remove crust from bread and spread mixture on each slice. Cut each slice in 3- or 4-inch strips.
4. Bake for 10 minutes or until crisp and lightly browned.

Yield: About 6 dozen

Zucchini Sticks

3-4 medium zucchini,
cut into 2-inch lengths
Vegetable oil for frying
4 eggs
¼ cup whipping cream
¼ teaspoon salt
½ teaspoon freshly ground pepper
¾ cup seasoned bread crumbs

1. Slice zucchini into french fry-sized sticks. Preheat oven to 350º if using a fryer or electric skillet, otherwise cover bottom of fry pan with oil and heat until hot (when hot, pan will sizzle when sprinkled with water).
2. Whisk together eggs, whipping cream, salt and pepper in a bowl. Dip zucchini pieces into egg mixture, then coat with breadcrumbs. Add to hot oil in batches and fry until brown and crisp, about 3 to 4 minutes. Drain on paper toweling.
3. Serve hot.

Yield: 4 servings

Pecan-Honey Mustard Chicken Wings

½ cup butter
½ cup honey
4 tablespoons Dijon-style mustard
1½ cups pecans, finely chopped
2 cups fresh fine bread crumbs
4 pounds chicken wings and drumsticks

1. In a small saucepan, melt butter. Whisk in honey and mustard, simmer, stirring occasionally, for about 5 minutes. Set aside to cool slightly.
2. Combine pecans and fresh bread crumbs. Set aside. Remove and discard tips from wings. Cut wings into two pieces and place in a large shallow dish. Pour butter mixture over wings and stir to coat completely. Roll wings in crumb mixture and place in single layer in a large foil-lined baking dish.
3. Bake at 350º for 15 minutes.

Yield: 4 dozen

Cook's Note:
If reheating is necessary, bake at 400º for 15 minutes. Wings may be frozen after baking. Reheat while still frozen for 30 minutes at 350º.

What is a Fluffernutter?

The prime ingredients in a fluffernutter are peanut butter and marshmallow fluff. Fluff is like a soft marshmallow. Archibald Query of Somerville made the first fluff in his kitchen and sold it door-to-door. In 1920, he sold the recipe to H. Allen Durkee and Fred Mauer for $500. This product has created generations of children and adults who are true devotees of the product. Years ago, a friend's daughter and I made a fluffernutter pizza — it wasn't bad!

Hot Cocoa

5 tablespoons cocoa
4 tablespoons sugar
½ cup water
1 quart milk
½ teaspoon vanilla extract
Fluff or tiny marshmallows

1. Dissolve sugar in water over medium heat.
2. Increase heat to medium high. Add cocoa and bring to boil. Cook and stir for 3 minutes.
3. Lower heat to medium, add milk and heat just to the boiling point (do not boil). Beat with a rotary beater or whisk until frothy. Add vanilla.
4. Top each cup with a teaspoon of fluff or a few tiny marshmallows.

Yield: 5 (5-ounce) servings

Cook's Note:
Growing up, my brother and I were served a cup of hot cocoa with fluff floating on top when we came inside from skating or sledding. Cocoa was always a family favorite before going to bed in the winter. I can still see my mother at the stove with her special hot cocoa pan, cooking and stirring our drink.

A Museum Dedicated to Moss

For over a century, Irish immigrants gathered carrageen, a seaweed-like product used in jellies, lotions and medicines. It has only been in recent years that this practice was abandoned. At the Maritime and Irish Mossing Museum in Scituate, visitors can observe the tools of the trade that were used to gather moss and learn about the industry. In addition, museum visitors will also find interesting artifacts and stories about the River of a Thousand Ships.

In today's high-tech world, we often forget that Massachusetts was a state where many of its citizens earned their living from the sea.

Mulled Cider

Early American recipes for mulled cider called for steeping the sugar and spices for several days, pouring into pewter cups and then heating by inserting a red hot poker into the cider. Today, we simply put the cider in a large pot on the stove.

1 gallon cider
1 cup brown sugar
2 teaspoons whole cloves
2 teaspoons whole allspice
8 sticks cinnamon
Grated nutmeg

1. Place cloves, allspice and cinnamon in cheesecloth and tie.
2. Put spice bag and add sugar in cider. Simmer for 15 minutes.
3. Strain and serve hot.

Yield: 16 to 20 servings

Cook's Note:
I prefer to use less sugar and still find it plenty sweet. Fresh cider is sweet enough, especially at the beginning of the season in late September and early October.

Massachusetts' First Elected President

John Adams, the second president of the United States, was born in Quincy on October 30, 1735. In 1797, he became president and was the first president to live in the White House. In 1800, he lost his reelection campaign to Thomas Jefferson. After his defeat, he returned home to Quincy where he continued his many interests. Over the years, Adams' relationship with Jefferson was strained, but the men did communicate. On July 4, 1826, he whispered his last words to his wife and family, "Thomas Jefferson survives", not knowing that Jefferson has passed away at Monticello a few hours earlier.

Today, engraved in the fireplace in the State Dining Room at the White House is a quote from a letter written by Adams to his wife, Abigail, "I pray Heaven to bestow the best of blessings on this house and all that shall hereafter inhabit it. May none but honest and wise men ever rule under this roof."

Cranberry Fruit Punch

2 quarts cranberry juice
2 cups orange juice
2 cans frozen strawberry-lemon juice
3 cups pineapple juice
2 cups water
1 frozen ice mold

1. Chill all ingredients before mixing.
2. Mix ingredients in a large punch bowl. Dip mold quickly into hot water to loosen. Place frozen mold in bowl.
3. Garnish with lemon, lime and orange.

Yield: 20 (4-ounce) servings

Chef's Note: Fill ring mold with water and add a few slices of lime, lemon and strawberries.

Party Punch

1 large can pineapple juice
½ gallon orange juice
½ cup sugar
1 cup lemon juice
1 (2-liter) bottle ginger ale, chilled
2 quarts sherbet (any flavor)

1. Combine pineapple and orange juice in a large punch bowl.
2. Mix sugar and lemon juice until sugar is dissolved. Add to juices and blend.
3. Just before serving, add ginger ale and sherbet.

Yield: 40 (4-ounce) servings

Cook's Note:
The sherbet makes the punch sweet enough, but feel free to adjust the amount of sugar used to your own taste. If at all possible, use freshly squeezed orange juice — it really makes a difference.

Champagne Punch

2 bottles champagne, chilled
1 cup brandy
1 cup Cointreau
1 liter bottle club soda, chilled

Combine all ingredients in a large punch bowl with lots of ice. Quality of taste depends of quality of product used.

Yield: 1 quart

Blueberry Smoothie

¾ cup skim milk
⅓ cup orange juice
¾ cup lowfat vanilla yogurt
1½ pints fresh blueberries
⅓ cup banana, sliced
¾ cup ice cubes

1. In a blender combine milk, orange juice, yogurt, blueberries, banana and ice.
2. Blend on medium speed until smooth enough to drink. Smoothie will still contain small bits of blueberries.

Old Ironsides

Ay, tear her tattered ensign down!
Long has it waved on high,
And many an eye has danced to see
That banner in the sky…

In 1830, it was erroneously reported that the U.S. Navy was going to scrap the vessel Old Ironsides. This led Oliver Wendell Holmes to write the above poem. Old Ironsides is the nickname for the USS Constitution, the oldest commissioned warship afloat in the world. The poem, along with public outcry, saved the famous frigate from demise.

Old Ironsides got her name because bullets could not penetrate her seven-inch tough oak sides. Built from 1794-1797 at the Edmund Hartt's shipyard in Boston, the ship last saw battle in the War of 1812; never in her long career did she lose a battle. In 1998, a celebration of naval vessels and tall ships from around the world descended on Boston Harbor to honor the USS Constitution and participate in its 200th birthday party. She is currently in berth at the Charlestown Naval Yard.

Irish Coffee

1 ounce Kahlúa liqueur
1 ounce Irish whiskey
1 cup hot black coffee
Fresh whipped cream
Ground nutmeg

1. Put the Kahlúa into a heated mug or stemmed goblet.
2. Add whiskey and hot coffee, and stir.
3. Add a dollop of whipped cream and sprinkle with nutmeg.

Yield: 1 serving

Breads and Brunch

Ashfield

Anna, Damn Her

As with so many New England foods, there is a story behind the name Anadama. Whether it is true or not doesn't matter; it adds a bit of mystery. The story goes that a fisherman, whose name is lost to history, had a lazy wife and as a consequence he had to do all his own cooking and baking. He named the bread after her, "Anna, damn her," and over time it got shortened to Anadama. However the bread got its name, it is delicious.

Anadama Bread

2 cups boiling water
½ cup cornmeal
½ cup shortening
⅓ cup sugar
⅓ cup molasses
Package dry yeast
¼ cup lukewarm water
1 tablespoon sugar
5-6 cups flour
2 teaspoons salt

1. Combine boiling water, cornmeal and shortening in a large mixing bowl.
2. Let mixture cool, then add the sugar and molasses.
3. Dissolve the dry yeast, and tablespoon of sugar into lukewarm water. When dissolved, add to cornmeal mixture.
4. Gradually beat in the flour and salt.
5. Turn out on floured board and knead until dough is smooth and elastic. Put in greased bowl, rolling dough until it is coated. Cover with damp cloth and let stand until doubled in bulk.
6. Punch down and shape into two loaves (or pan rolls). Place in greased pans, cover and let stand again until doubled in bulk.
7. Preheat oven and bake bread at 375° for 45 to 50 minutes. The rolls are baked for 20 to 25 minutes.

America's Oldest Library

The Boston Public Library, located in Copley Square, is America's oldest public library. In 1848, it was revolutionary to allow people to borrow books without a charge. In addition to a collection of over eight million books, the Library is also known for its vast art collection. There are works by Winslow Homer, Augustus Saint-Gaudens, John Singleton Copley, John James Audubon, Rembrandt, Picasso, Tousouse-Lautrec and John Singer Sargent.

In 1890, John Singer Sargent agreed to paint two murals in the Library. He used a variety of mediums including metal, paper and jewels. His subject was the history of religion.

Pumpkin Bread

4 cups all-purpose flour
3 cups sugar
2 teaspoons baking soda
1½ teaspoons salt
1 teaspoon baking powder
1 teaspoon cinnamon
1 teaspoon nutmeg
1 teaspoon allspice
½ teaspoon ground clove
1 cup vegetable oil
1 (14-ounce) can pumpkin
¾ cup cold water
4 eggs

1. Preheat oven to 350°. Grease either two large loaf pans or four small ones.
2. In a large bowl place flour, sugar, baking soda, salt, powder, and spices. Mix thoroughly.
3. Make a well in the center of the flour. Pour in vegetable oil, pumpkin and water. Mix well.
4. Add eggs, one at a time, blend well.
5. Pour into loaf pans.

Chef's Note:
This recipe also makes delicious muffins. For a different taste, add dried cranberries to batter.

Tea or Polo

Originating in 1893, the Wenham Village Improvement Society's mission was to raise funds to support projects in the Village. Originally, they raised money to install street lights, signs and create plantings to beautify the town. Over the years, hundreds of thousands of dollars have been raised by the organization.

For an area better known for its old estates, polo games and fox hunts, the Wenham Tea Room has been serving lunch and tea for nearly one hundred years. It is a great place to dine when touring the North Shore or after a polo match at the nearby Myopia Hunt Club. You will definitely be taken back to a quieter gentler time...not such a bad thing in this day and age.

Cranberry Bread

2 tablespoons butter
1 cup sugar
1 tablespoon orange peel, grated
¾ cup orange juice
1 egg, beaten
2 cups all-purpose flour
1½ teaspoons baking powder
1 teaspoon salt
½ teaspoon baking soda
1 cup fresh cranberries

1. Preheat oven to 350º. Grease and flour a large loaf pan or 12-cup muffin tin.
2. Cream butter and sugar in large bowl. Add orange peel, juice and egg. Mix well.
3. In separate bowl sift flour, baking powder, salt and baking soda. Gradually add to large bowl, beating until smooth. Do not overbeat.
4. Stir in the cranberries. Pour into either loaf pan or muffin tin.
5. Bake bread for 55 minutes or muffins for 30 minutes. Check with tester to make sure bread is done.

Portuguese Sweet Bread

2 packages active dry yeast
¼ cup warm water
1 cup milk, scalded
¾ cup sugar
1 teaspoon salt
3 eggs
½ cup butter
5½-6 cups all-purpose flour
1 teaspoon sugar for egg wash
1 egg for egg wash

1. Dissolve yeast in warm water in a bowl. Scald milk and soften butter in milk while milk cools.
2. Stir into yeast cooled milk mixture, salt, eggs, sugar and three cups of flour. Beat until smooth. Stir in enough remaining flour to make dough easy to handle.
3. Turn the dough out on lightly floured surface and knead until smooth and elastic (about 5 minutes). Place in greased bowl, turning once to grease top, cover and let rise to double bulk in warm place (1½ to 2 hours).
4. Punch down, divide in half. Shape into slightly flat round loaf and place in greased round layer cake pan 9x1½-inch. Cover and let rise until double in bulk (about 1 hour).
5. Beat one egg slightly and brush over top of loaves, sprinkle 1 teaspoon sugar over tops, and bake in preheated oven at 350º for 35 to 45 minutes until golden brown.

Yield: 2 loaves

Corn Bread

¾ cup sugar
2 eggs
¾ teaspoon salt
2 cups flour
1 cup yellow corn meal, granulated
1 tablespoon baking powder
1 tablespoon butter, melted
1½ cups milk

1. Preheat oven to 350º. Grease and flour the interior of an 8x10-inch baking pan.
2. Beat eggs and sugar together. Sift flour, corn meal, baking powder and salt into mixture.
3. Add milk and melted butter.
4. Quickly mix the batter and pour into baking pan.

Yield: 20 (2-inch) squares

Will He Ever Return?

"No, he'll never return and his fate is still unlearned. He may ride forever beneath the streets of Boston, he's the man who never returned." Made famous by the musical group the Kingston Trio, this song refers to the infamous MBTA subway system of Boston. What few know is that Boston is the birthplace of the American mass transportation system. It began in 1630 as a ferry service operated by Thomas Williams, who ferried people from Charlestown to Chelsea and then on to Boston. According to the MBTA, Boston's transit system is the oldest and fourth largest in the nation and has a history longer than that of American independence.

Irish Soda Bread

2½ cups flour
2 teaspoons baking powder
½ teaspoon baking soda
¼ cup butter
½ cup sugar
1 egg beaten
1½ cups buttermilk
1 cup raisins
1 teaspoon caraway seeds
1 tablespoons butter, melted
Sugar

1. Preheat oven to 350°. Grease and flour a round cake pan.
2. Mix flour, baking powder, baking soda together.
3. Cream butter and sugar together; add egg.
4. Gradually add flour to butter mixture alternating with buttermilk. Stir in raisins and caraway seeds.
5. Fill loaf pan , three-quarters full. Cut slit in top. Brush top with melted butter and sprinkle with sugar.
6. Bake at 350° for 30 minutes, then lower temperature to 325° and continue baking for an additional 30 minutes.

Yield: 1 loaf

Parker House

In 1855, one of Boston's famous landmarks opened for business. Hotelier Harvey Parker finally fulfilled his dream of building a first class European-style hotel in the heart of Boston. The Parker House, now known as the Omni Parker House, is the longest continuously operating hotel in the United States. It is from the kitchen of this great hotel that we have the Parker House rolls.

Parker House Rolls

2 cups scalded milk
2 teaspoon salt
3 tablespoons unsalted butter
2 tablespoons sugar
1 yeast cake dissolved in
¼ cup lukewarm water
Flour
2 tablespoons melted butter

1. Preheat oven to 375º.
2. Add butter, sugar and salt to scalded milk. When lukewarm, add dissolved yeast cake and three cups of flour to make a slightly sticky dough that forms a ball.
3. Butter a large bowl. Knead dough on a lightly floured surface, kneading in more all-purpose flour (about 2½ cups) if dough is too sticky, about 10 minutes, or until smooth and elastic but still slightly sticky. Form into a ball and put in buttered bowl. Turn to coat with butter, then let rise in bowl, covered with plastic wrap, in a warm place for one hour or until doubled in bulk.
4. Butter a 13x9-inch baking dish. Divide dough into 20 equal pieces and roll into balls. Arrange evenly in greased baking dish and let rise, covered loosely, in a warm place 45 minutes, or until almost doubled in bulk.
5. Make a deep crease through the middle of each piece with knife handle or other round object such as a chopstick; brush over one-half with melted butter, fold, and press edges together. Let rolls rise, covered loosely for 15 minutes.
6. Bake in the middle of oven until golden, about 12 to 15 minutes. Let rolls cool in pan on a rack for 5 minutes.

Hassanamisco Indian Reservation

Imagine a piece of land in Massachusetts that has never been sold or traded. Such a parcel of 4.5 acres can be found in the Central Massachusetts town of Grafton. The name Hassanamisco means place of small stones. The Hassanamisco Indian Reservation is the smallest and oldest reservation in Massachusetts, and the third smallest in the United States. Owned by the Nipmuc Tribal Council of the Hassanamisco band, the reservation is open to the public during the summer during the tribal meetings. An annual powwow is held on the last Sunday in July and attracts Native Peoples from all over the area.

Lavender Popovers

Lavender tours and gardening are very popular in Massachusetts. In Harwich, you have the beautiful fields of the Cape Cod Lavender Farm and at the end of each June, the Lavender Growers of Franklin County have a wonderful tour.

4 eggs
1 cup all-purpose flour
¾ cup milk
2 tablespoons lavender blossoms

1. Preheat over to 375°.
2. Using ½ teaspoon for each, butter 12 popover pans or muffin cups and set aside.
3. Place popover or muffins pan in oven to heat. Be careful not to burn butter.
4. Whisk together eggs, flour and milk; stir in blossoms.
5. Remove hot pan from oven and pour batter making sure each pan is about ¾ full.
6. Bake in oven for about 35 minutes or until puffed and golden.
7. Serve hot with butter and raspberry jam. The raspberry jam is a wonderful complement to the lavender in the popovers.

Lilac Sunday

Imagine a bright sunny spring day dedicated to the flowering shrub, the lilac. Each May both gardening enthusiasts and simply those who want to stroll in the sun come to visit the Arnold Arboretum of Harvard University to take in the scents of thousands of blooming lilacs.

Founded in 1872, the Arnold Arboretum is the country's oldest arboretum and home to over 15,000 species of woody plants, trees, shrubs and vines gathered from around the world. Designed by Frederick Law Olmsted, the 265-acre park, located in the Jamaica Plain section of Boston, is interlaced with walks and drives. It is also part of the Emerald Necklace park system.

Blueberry Cream Cheese Coffee Cake

2¼ cups flour
1 cup sugar
¾ cup butter
1½ teaspoons baking powder
¼ teaspoon salt
¾ cup sour cream
2 large eggs
1 teaspoon almond extract
1 (8-ounce) package cream cheese
2 cups blueberries
½ cup slivered almonds

1. Preheat oven to 350°. Lightly grease and flour a springform pan.
2. Mix flour and ¾ cup sugar; cut in butter. Add baking powder, salt, sour cream, one egg and the almond extract. Reserve one cup to sprinkle over top.
3. Press dough on bottom and up 2 inches on sides of pan.
4. In small bowl, beat cream cheese, remaining sugar and egg until well blended. Pour over dough. Arrange blueberries on top.
5. Mix remaining almonds with reserved crumb mixture and spread over top.
6. Bake 50 to 55 minutes.

Schooner Ernestina

In 1894, a new schooner named the Effie M. Morrissey was launched from the James & Tarr Yard in Gloucester. The ship began its illustrious career as a fishing schooner on the Grand Banks. It was also an Arctic expeditionary vessel under the command of Captain Robert Abram Bartlett and a World War II survey vessel under Commander Alexander Forbes.

After a galley fire in 1947, the ship was restored and its name changed to the Ernestina. It spent the next 35 years as a transatlantic packet, carrying passengers and goods between Cape Verde and the United States. In 1982, the Republic of Cape Verde gave the schooner to the people of the United States. Today, the Ernestina is a National Historic Landmark. It is one of the last of six remaining schooners built in Essex and the official vessel of the Commonwealth of Massachusetts.

Strawberry Muffins

½ cup butter, softened
1 cup sugar
2 eggs
2 cups flour
2 teaspoons baking powder
¼ teaspoon salt
⅔ cup milk
1 teaspoon grated lemon rind
1 cup fresh strawberries, chopped
1 tablespoon cinnamon sugar

1. Preheat oven to 375°. Grease or line muffin pans.
2. Cream butter in large bowl; gradually add sugar and eggs, creaming until light and fluffy.
3. Sift together flour, baking powder and salt. Add to creamed mixture alternately with milk, beginning and ending with dry ingredients.
4. Stir in lemon rind and fold in berries.
5. Spoon batter into muffin pans, filling each ⅔ full. Sprinkle sugar lightly over top of batter. Bake 18 to 20 minutes.

Yield: 12 muffins

Bookstores Galore!

Looking for a good book? Then go no further than the city of Cambridge, located on the banks of the Charles River. Cambridge, home to Harvard University and Radcliffe College, is second only to the country of Wales in the number of bookstores per capita in the world. However, if you were to compare bookstores on a square-mile basis, there is little doubt that Cambridge wins hands down.

Apple-Cider Bread or Muffins

1 cup butter
1½ cups sugar
3 eggs
4 cups flour
1½ tablespoons baking powder
1½ teaspoons salt
1½ teaspoons cinnamon
2 cups apple cider
2 cups apples, peeled, cored and chopped
1 teaspoon cinnamon

1. Preheat oven to 375°.
2. Grease and flour two loaf pans or 18 muffin cups.
3. Cream butter and 1¼ cups sugar together in a large bowl. Add eggs and cream thoroughly.
4. Sift the dry ingredients together. Add them to the egg mixture, alternating with the apple cider. Stir in the chopped apples.
5. Divide the batter between the prepared loaf pan (or fill muffin cups ⅔ full).
6. Combine the remaining ¼ cup sugar with the cinnamon in a small bowl, and sprinkle it over the batter.
7. Bake for 50 to 70 minutes for bread (30 to 40 minutes for muffins), or until a toothpick inserted in the center comes out clean.

Yield: 2 loaves or 18 muffins

Spaceship or Department Store?

From the 1940s through the early 1990s, the department stores of Massachusetts had wonderful restaurants. It was an adventure to go downtown to shop. The Jordan Marsh flagship store was located on Washington Street in downtown Boston (now Macy's). I was introduced to these delicious blueberry muffins at Shoppers World in Framingham. This spaceship-design Jordan Marsh store was unique. Regretfully, the landmark store is now gone.

Jordan Marsh's Blueberry Muffins

½ cup butter
1 cup sugar
2 eggs
1 teaspoon vanilla
2 cups flour
2 teaspoon baking powder
½ teaspoon salt
½ cup milk
2½ cups medium blueberries

1. Preheat oven to 375°.
2. Cream butter and sugar.
3. Add eggs and vanilla. Beat well.
4. Add sifted dry ingredients alternately with milk.
5. Fold in berries.
6. Fill greased or papered tins almost to the top. Bake for 30 minutes.

Chef's Note:
If using large cultivated blueberries, use fewer blueberries.

Source: former Jordan Marsh
Framingham

Lemon-Raspberry Muffins

2¼ cups all-purpose flour
½ cup sugar
2½ teaspoons baking powder
½ teaspoon salt
1 (8-ounce) container lemon yogurt
1 (6-ounce) package of fresh or frozen (thawed) raspberries
½ cup vegetable oil
2 large eggs
1 teaspoon grated lemon rind
3 tablespoons sugar
1 tablespoon cold butter

1. Preheat oven to 375°. Lightly grease muffins tins.
2. Combine 2 cups flour, sugar, baking powder and salt in a large bowl.
3. Make a well in center of mixture. Stir together yogurt, vegetable oil and eggs; add to dry ingredients, stirring until just moistened.
4. Toss together 2 tablespoons of flour and raspberries; fold gently into batter. Fill muffin tins ⅔ full.
5. Combine remaining 2 tablespoons flour and 3 tablespoons sugar; cut butter into mixture until mixture is crumbly. Sprinkle over batter.
6. Bake for 20 to 25 minutes until golden. Remove muffins from pan and cool.

Yield: 12 muffins

Pineapple Muffins

1 (8.25-ounce) can crushed pineapple
Milk
1½ cups packaged biscuit mix
4 tablespoons sugar
1 egg, beaten
1 tablespoon orange peel, finely shredded

1. Preheat oven to 400°.
2. Drain pineapple, reserving syrup. Add enough milk to syrup to measure ¾ cup.
3. Combine biscuit mix and 3 tablespoons sugar.
4. Combine egg, reserved pineapple syrup and ¼ cup of drained pineapple. Add to dry ingredients, stirring just until moistened. Do not overmix.
5. Fill greased or papered muffin tins ⅔ full.
6. Combine remaining pineapple, 1 tablespoon sugar and orange peel. Spoon 1 tablespoon of mixture on top of each muffin. Bake for 20 to 25 minutes or until golden.

Yield: 8 to 10 muffins

Brimfield Antique Show

Three times a year the quiet town of Brimfield becomes the destination for antique lovers from around the world when it hosts the largest outdoor antique show in New England.

Whether a serious dealer or a casual browser, nearly 25,000 potential buyers and sellers walk along a one-mile stretch of Route 20 to visit the fields filled with thousands of dealers. Visit the show in May, July and September each year to find those special and irresistible treasures you always wanted.

Citrus and Cranberry Scones

⅔ cup butter, room temperature
⅓ cup sugar
Grated zest of 1 orange
1⅔ cups sour cream
2 cups plus 2 tablespoons cake flour
2 tablespoons baking powder
2 cups plus 2 tablespoons pastry flour
¼ cup dried cranberries

1. Preheat oven to 350°.
2. In a large bowl, cream butter until light and fluffy. Add sugar and orange zest and mix to obtain a very light consistency. Stir in the sour cream until well combined.
3. In a medium bowl, stir together cake flour, baking powder and pastry flour. Stir flour mixture and cranberries into the butter substitute and continue mixing until just combined – do not overmix.
4. On a floured work surface, roll dough out to ¾-inch thickness. Using a 2-inch round biscuit cutter, cut the dough into 20 rounds and place on ungreased baking sheets.
5. Bake in center of preheated oven for 15 to 20 minutes, or until golden brown. Let cool slightly on wire racks before serving.

Steiger's Tea Room Holiday Stollen

Steiger's was a wonderful department store located in Springfield, but like Jordan Marsh in Boston, it did not survive the move of the population to the suburbs and the shopping malls.

2½ cups sifted flour
¾ cup sugar
4 teaspoons baking powder
½ teaspoon salt
¼ teaspoon ground mace
⅛ teaspoon ground cardamom
½ cup margarine
1 cup creamed cottage cheese
1 egg
2 tablespoons light rum
¾ teaspoon vanilla extract
½ cup pecans, chopped
¼ cup raisins or dried cranberries
¼ cup candied fruit
3 tablespoons melted margarine
2 tablespoons sugar
¼ teaspoon vanilla

1. Combine the first six ingredients. Cut margarine into mixture with blender or two knives until mixture resembles coarse meal.
2. Into a small mixing bowl, combine cottage cheese, egg, rum and vanilla. Beat at medium speed for two minutes, scraping bowl occasionally. Stir in chopped nuts, raisins and candied fruit.
3. Add to flour mixture and mix until ingredients are moistened. Form dough into a ball.
4. On a lightly floured board, knead slightly for about 10 turns. Roll dough to form an 8x10-inch oval. Lightly crease dough just off center, parallel to the 10-inch side.
5. Brush dough with 1 tablespoon melted margarine. Fold small section over larger section on crease. Cover ungreased baking sheet with brown or parchment paper. Place dough on paper.
6. Bake at 350° for about 45 minutes. Brush with remaining margarine.
7. Combine 2 tablespoons sugar and ¼ teaspoon vanilla; mix well and sprinkle on top of stollen.
8. Remove from baking sheet and cool on rack. Decorate with candied cherries, if desired.

Around the World By Ship and Space Shuttle

On September 30, 1787, the ship Columbia set sail from Boston for China. Since there were no Panama or Suez canals, she sailed south around Cape Horn of South America up to the northwest coast of the United States and then on to Canton (now Shanghai). Upon leaving China, the Columbia headed west around the Cape of Hope in South Africa returning to Boston on August 9, 1790 – after an absence of three years and sailing over 49,000 miles. The Columbia was the first American vessel to sail around the world. Two hundred years later her namesake, the space shuttle Columbia, circled the globe hundreds of miles above the earth.

Potato Brunch Casserole

1 (32-ounce) package of hash brown
1 pint whipping cream
1 (16-ounce) package of Swiss cheese, grated
¼ pound butter (1 stick)
Paprika

1. Preheat oven to 350°.
2. Put all ingredients in an oven-to-table casserole dish and mix thoroughly.
3. Bake covered for 30 minutes. Remove cover and continue baking for an additional 30 minutes until golden and bubbly.

Cook's Note:
Do not double recipe in same pan.

The Gingerbread House

In the 1930s, Santarella was built as the studio of Sir Henry Hudson Kitson who sculpted the famous Minuteman statue in Lexington. The studio roof was designed to represent the rolling hills of the Berkshires in the autumn. It weighs over 80 tons and while made of modern roofing materials, it simulates a thatched roof. Santarella is located in the town of Tyringham.

Gingerbread Waffles

Growing up, waffles were a traditional Sunday night supper. They make a wonderful treat for supper, brunch or even Christmas morning.

2 cups all-purpose flour
1 teaspoon ground ginger
½ teaspoon ground cinnamon
¼ teaspoon ground cloves
½ teaspoon salt
1 teaspoon baking soda
1 teaspoon baking powder
¼ cup sugar
3 eggs, separated
½ cup molasses
1½ cups nonfat buttermilk
1 stick butter or margarine, melted

1. Heat waffle iron. Warm oven to 200º.
2. In a large bowl, sift together dry ingredients.
3. In a medium bowl, whisk together egg yolks, molasses, buttermilk, and butter. Pour into dry ingredients and stir until just combined. Do not over stir as this will make for tough waffles.
4. In medium bowl beat egg whites until stiff, but not dry. Fold into batter.
5. Ladle about ½ cup batter onto each section of the waffle grill. Spread batter almost to edge.
6. Close lid and bake about 5 minutes until no steam emerges from the iron.
7. Transfer cooked waffles to ovenproof container or cookie sheet and place in warmed oven until ready to serve. Keep covered with tin foil so waffles don't dry out.
8. Dust with confectioners sugar and serve with warm maple syrup. Tasty with sliced fruit spread on top of waffles. You can also serve with whipped cream.

Yield: 8 servings

Salem Witch Trials

In 1692 in a quiet town north of Boston, the unusual behavior of two young girls launched the Salem Witch Trials. When the girls, daughter and niece of Revered Samuel Parris of Salem Village, became ill and did not improve, the village doctor, William Griggs, was contacted. After an examination, he declared that the girls were bewitched. This statement led to the trials, conviction and subsequent executions of nineteen individuals. Many years later, the jurors and magistrates apologized and restitution was made to the victims' families.

Hot Apple Oatmeal

4 cups milk
2 tablespoons butter
½ teaspoon salt
½ teaspoon cinnamon
1 cup raisins or dried cranberries
2 cups chopped apple
2 cups rolled oats
Raw or brown sugar

1. Combine milk and oats with salt and let them sit for an hour or overnight.
2. When ready to cook, add more milk if necessary, along with brown sugar, butter, salt, cinnamon, apples, and raisins or cranberries in a saucepan and heat thoroughly, stirring constantly.
3. Place into individual cereal bowls and sprinkle top with raw or brown sugar before serving.

Yield: 4 servings

Cook's Note:
If using dried cranberries, add them in step 1. This allows the cranberries to soften and plump.

Organ of Muskets

This is the Arsenal. From floor to ceiling,
Like a huge organ, rise the burnished arms;
But from their silent pipes no anthem pealing
Startles the villages with strange alarms.

Henry Wadsworth Longfellow

In 1777, the Arsenal at Springfield was established to manufacture weapons for the American Revolution. The site was chosen because of Springfield's strategic location at the intersection of highways and the Connecticut River. In 1794, President Washington selected Springfield as one of two federal armories, the other being at Harpers Ferry. The armory is famous for its Springfield Rifle and the M1 rifle. After two centuries of providing America's military with the finest weapons, the armory was closed in 1968 upon orders from the U.S. Department of Defense. While the National Park Service now operates the armory museum, the site has found a second purpose. It is now the home to Springfield Technical Community College, the Springfield Technology Park and the Springfield Enterprise Center, an entrepreneurial incubator.

Ambrosia

6 red grapefruit, peeled, seeded, sectioned
6 navel oranges, peel, seeded, sectioned
½ cup flaked coconut
Maraschino cherries, halved

Remove the white pith from the fruit. Mix sections with coconut and cherries. Serve chilled.

Yield: 8 servings

Green Eggs and Ham

Springfield is the birthplace of the *Cat in the Hat* and its author Theodore Geisel, better known to millions around the world as Dr. Seuss. In 2002, a wonderful memorial opened at the museum at the Quadrangle to honor this marvelous storyteller. A bronze sculpture of Dr. Seuss is surrounded by many of his most memorable characters — the Grinch and his dog Max; Horton the elephant; Thidwick the bighearted moose; the Lorax, Gertrude McFuzz, Things One and Two; and Yertle the turtle, including a garden with a 10-turtle-tall tower above a granite reflecting pool. What a terrific spot to spend a sunny afternoon! The only thing missing is a plate of green eggs and ham.

Sausage and Egg Breakfast Casserole

1½ pounds mild pork sausage
3-4 slices bread, trimmed and cubed
1 (6-ounce) package Cheddar cheese
9 large eggs
3 cups milk
1½ teaspoons dry mustard
1 teaspoon salt
Dash pepper

1. Cook sausage in skillet over medium heat until it is no longer pink. Break up sausage with wooden spoon into small pieces. Drain well.
2. Arrange bread cubes in bottom of a lightly greased 13x9-inch baking dish. Top with sausage and cheese.
3. Whisk together eggs, milk, mustard and seasonings; pour evenly over cheese. Cover and chill 8 hours or overnight.
4. Remove from refrigerator 30 minutes before ready to cook. Preheat oven to 350° and bake for 45 minutes or until set.

Yield: 8 to 10 servings

French King Bridge Named for King Louis XIV

Sitting 140 feet above the Connecticut River, the French King Bridge in Gill was constructed in 1932. It cost only $385,000 and took twelve months to build. Crews worked from both sides of the river towards the middle. In 1750, the French King Rock served as a landmark for French and Indian scouting parties who named it in honor of King Louis XIV.

The scenic views from the bridge looking north towards Vermont and New Hampshire or south towards Connecticut are spectacular. Visitors can park and walk across the bridge to enjoy the views or take a ride up the River on the Quinnetukut II, which departs from Northfield Mountain Recreational Area.

Over the years, several groups including the Commonwealth of Massachusetts, Northeast Utilities and a variety of non-profit organizations, have purchased the land on the riverbanks to protect it from development.

Apple Cheese Omelet

4 eggs
2 tablespoons Parmesan cheese, freshly grated
1 green apple, peeled and thinly sliced
2 ounces Roquefort cheese, crumbled
2 tablespoons butter
Salt and pepper to taste

1. Beat eggs with Parmesan cheese, salt and pepper.
2. Sauté apple slices in 1 tablespoon butter to heat apples. Remove apples.
3. Cook eggs in remaining butter, as soon as omelet is set, spread the apple slices over one half of omelet and place Roquefort cheese on top. Fold over other half of omelet. Serve hot.

Cook's Note:
Substituting Saga Blue or Gorgonzola cheese are equally as delicious.

The Deerfield Inn

Located in the center of the 350-year-old National Historic Landmark village of Deerfield, the Deerfield Inn has been in operation since 1884. It opened at the same time as a plague of grasshoppers was eating its way across Franklin County. This event did not deter the many guests who came to while away the summer in the country.

In the early years, guests arrived by stagecoach, carriages and on horseback. As technology grew, guests began arriving by trolley and eventually the automobile. In a brochure from 1885, the Inn is described as "in all appointments far ahead of the average country inn." The Inn has changed little over the years and it remains a wonderful place to spend some leisure time.

Banana Bread French Toast

2 large bananas
2 cups flour
1 teaspoon baking soda
1 teaspoon baking powder
1 cup sugar
½ cup oil
2 eggs
1 ounce milk
1 teaspoon vanilla
1 cup pecans, chopped (optional)
6 eggs
1 cup half & half
¼ teaspoon cinnamon
1 teaspoon vanilla
Pinch salt

1. Preheat oven to 350º.
2. Mash bananas in bowl; mix all dry ingredients, except sugar, in another bowl.
3. Mix in sugar, oil and eggs to bananas. Mix well; add vanilla and milk.
4. Add dry ingredients to wet ingredients, then add nuts.
5. Pour into a greased, floured 4x8-inch loaf pan. Bake 45 minutes or until a tester comes out clean.
6. For french toast, whisk eggs, half & half, cinnamon, vanilla and salt vigorously.
7. Slice bread ½-inch thick, dip into French toast batter and carefully place onto a hot, buttered griddle.
8. Cook 2 to 3 minutes until golden brown. Turn over and cook for another 1 to 2 minutes.
9. Serve garnished with fresh fruit and sprinkle with confectioner's sugar. Top with warm maple syrup.

Source: Deerfield Inn
Deerfield

Johnny Appleseed

The man credited with establishing apple orchards throughout the Midwest was born in Leominster and spent part of his youth in Longmeadow. John Chapman, also known as Johnny Appleseed, started nurseries by planting apple seeds purchased from cider mills. He led a very simple life. After his death at age 75, it was learned that he owned and leased considerable land planted with, what else but, apples.

Bickford's Apple Pancakes

1 cup unbleached bread flour
½ cup powdered sugar
⅛ teaspoon nutmeg
Dash salt
6 tablespoons light cream
2 eggs

For each pancake:
2 tablespoons butter
½ cup thin sliced apples, blanched
2 tablespoons cinnamon mix

Cinnamon Mix:
1 teaspoon cinnamon
¼ cup sugar

1. Preheat oven to 500°.
2. Mix dry ingredients; add cream and water, mix well.
3. Add eggs and fold lightly, just enough to break yolks.
4. Place butter in 9-inch round pan.
5. Put one-half of batter in pan; distribute apples on batter.
6. Bake until set, approximately 5 minutes.
7. When set, sprinkle with 2 tablespoons of cinnamon sugar mix on top and turn. Bake 10 minutes until edges are brown.
8. Serve with glazed cinnamon side up.

Yield: 2 pancakes

Sausage Ring with Cheese-Scrambled Eggs

12 eggs
1½ cups milk
1½ cups saltine crackers, crushed (approximately 42 crackers)
1 cup apple, peeled and chopped
¼ cup onion, chopped
2 pounds bulk pork sausage
3 tablespoons butter
3 tablespoons flour
1 cup small-curd cottage cheese

1. Beat together two eggs and ½ cup milk. Stir in cracker crumbs, apples, onion, and ¼ teaspoon pepper. Add sausage and mix well.
2. Firmly pack meat mixture into a 6½-cup ring mold. You can prepare sausage mixture, put in mold and refrigerate overnight before baking.
3. Carefully unmold sausage ring onto a rack in a shallow baking pan.
4. Bake in 350° oven for 50 minutes. Transfer to platter. Keep warm.
5. While sausage is cooking, melt butter in 3-quart saucepan. Blend in flour. Add remaining cup of milk all at once. Cook and stir over medium heat till bubbly.
6. Cook and stir 2 minutes. Beat together the remaining 10 eggs, the cheese, ½ teaspoon salt, and dash pepper. Stir into sauce.
7. Cook, stirring frequently, till eggs are firm, but moist. Spoon eggs into center of sausage ring.

Yield: 12 servings

Broiled Grapefruit

4 large pink grapefruits
8 teaspoons honey or red wine

1. Cut grapefruit in half, remove seeds and cut sections.
2. Sprinkle top of each half with brown sugar. Pour 1 teaspoon of honey on top of each halved grapefruit.
3. Place under broiler for few moments. Serve hot.

Yield: 8 (½ grapefruit) servings

The Art of Quilting

Quilts are an intrinsic part of the New England lifestyle. The art of quilting has experienced a resurgence in recent years. Many now collect the treasured memories of our history, and new quilts that will become heirlooms of the future are being created. The New England Quilt Museum in Lowell was founded by the New England Quilter's Guild. The museum preserves, interprets and celebrates American quilting past and present. The museum also offers changing exhibitions of contemporary, traditional and antique quilts.

Apple–Turkey Sausage Patties

1 onion, finely chopped
1½ cups tart apples, peeled and grated
1 pound ground turkey
2 large egg whites
1 cup fresh bread crumbs
1½ teaspoons salt
½ teaspoon freshly ground black pepper
½ teaspoon ground nutmeg
¼ teaspoon allspice
2 teaspoons dried sage

1. Coat a large nonstick skillet with cooking spray. Over medium heat sauté onions until soft, about 3 minutes. Add apples and continue sautéing for 3 to 5 minutes longer, or until apples are very tender.
2. Transfer to large bowl and let cool completely. Add turkey, breadcrumbs, egg whites, and spices; mix well.
3. Divide the sausage mixture into 16 (3-inch) patties.
4. Preheat oven to 450°. Spray baking sheet with nonstick cooking spray.
5. Bake patties until golden brown, about 10 minutes for fresh or 20 minutes for frozen. Turn halfway to insure even cooking.

Yield: 8 servings

Cook's Note: I recommend making the sausage 24 hours before cooking to let the seasonings mingle. Patties can be wrapped and stored in freezer for up to three months.

Soups and Salads

Old Deerfield

Firehouse or Art Center?

In a time when so many old buildings are torn down to make way for the new, it is nice to see one building restored not only to its original glory, but also given a new life. Originally built as a market house and lyceum in 1823, it served the citizens of Newburyport as a firehouse for over 100 years. After a new firehouse was built, the building lay waiting for its fate. Fortunately, a group created the Firehouse Center for the Arts and today it is the site of plays, concerts and other cultural events.

Cheeseburger Chowder

2 medium green peppers, chopped fine
1 onion, chopped fine
2 tablespoons flour
½ pound (8-ounces) hamburger
1 quart chicken broth
4 ounces cheddar cheese, shredded
1 pint half & half or milk

1. Sauté onions and peppers in large pot. Add hamburg and brown.
2. Add chicken broth. Mix flour with ¼ cup of broth and blend well before adding to mixture. Bring to a boil.
3. Add cheddar cheese and half & half (or milk). Stir until cheese is melted.
4. Season to taste. Serve hot with a salad and French bread.

Yield: 6 to 8 servings

Clam Chowder

1⅔ cups littleneck clams, cooked and chopped
1 garlic clove, chopped
1 cup water
2 ounces salt pork, or bacon, finely chopped,

1½ pounds potatoes, peeled and diced into ½-inch cubes
2 cups chopped onion
3 tablespoons flour
3 cups fish stock or clam juice
2 cups light cream

1. Clean clams by scrubbing shells. Place clams in a large pot along with the garlic and water. Steam the clams just until opened, about 6 to 20 minutes, depending upon their size. Drain and shell the clams, reserving the broth. Mince the clam flesh and set aside. Filter the clam broth either through coffee filters or cheesecloth and set aside.

2. In a large pot slowly render the salt port or bacon. Remove the cracklings or bacon and set them aside. Slowly cook the onions in the fat, stirring frequently until cooked, but not browned.

3. Stir in the flour and cook, stirring, for 3 minutes. Add the reserved clam broth and fish stock (use clam juice if fish stock is unavailable), and whisk to remove any flour lumps. Bring the liquid to a boil, add the potatoes, lower the heat, and simmer until the potatoes are cooked through, about 15 minutes.

4. Stir in the reserved clams, salt pork cracklings (or crumbled bacon), and light cream. Heat the chowder until it is the temperature you like, but do not let it boil. Serve in large soup bowls. Sprinkle with fresh chives and serve with oyster crackers.

Yield: 8 servings

Source: Legal Sea Foods
Boston

Silent Cal

Though Calvin Coolidge was born in Vermont on July 4, 1872, he graduated from Amherst College with honors. He then began practicing law in Massachusetts and started his career in politics as city councilman in Northampton and then as governor of the Commonwealth.

Coolidge often sat silently through interviews. His explanation for this was, "Many times I say only 'yes' or 'no' to people. Even that is too much. It winds them up for twenty minutes more." This legendary frugality with words earned him his nickname, Silent Cal. Upon leaving the White House, Coolidge retired to his home in Northampton where he passed away on January 5, 1933.

Marliave's Minestrone Soup

2 garlic cloves
¼ cup olive oil
¼ cup carrots, cut into ½-inch pieces
¼ cup celery, cut into ½-inch pieces
1 cup cabbage, cut into 1½-inch pieces
¼ cup green beans, 1½-inch pieces
¼ cup onions, cut into ½-inch pieces
2 quarts beef stock (boil 3 pounds beef bones for 2 hours, skim off fat and set aside)
1 cup fresh spinach
¼ cup peas
1 (28-ounce) can crushed tomatoes

1. In a large stock pot, brown garlic in oil. Add all vegetables except spinach and peas. Sauté until onions are translucent.
2. Add tomatoes and cook for 10 minutes.
3. Add beef stock, spinach and peas. Season with salt, pepper and oregano to taste.
4. Simmer for 30 minutes. Skim off fat, if necessary.

Yield: 8 servings

Source: Cafe Marliave
Boston

Baked Potato Soup

4 large baking potatoes
⅔ cup butter
⅔ cup flour
6 cups milk
¾ teaspoon salt
½ teaspoon pepper
4 green onions, chopped
12 slices bacon, crumbled
1¼ cups shredded Cheddar cheese
1 cup sour cream

1. Shrub the potatoes and prick each several times. Bake at 400º for about 1 hour or until soft to the touch. Cool completely. Cut the potatoes lengthwise into halves. Scoop out the pulp and set aside. Discard the skins.
2. Melt butter in a medium saucepan over low heat. Add the flour, stirring until smooth. Cook for one minute, stirring constantly.
3. Stir in the milk gradually. Cook over medium heat until thickened and bubbly, stirring constantly.
4. Add the potato pulp, salt, pepper, 2 green onions, ½ cup of bacon and 1 cup of cheese. Cook until heated through.
5. Stir in the sour cream. Heat gently, but do not boil. Stir in additional milk, if necessary, to achieve desired thickness.
6. Serve topped with the remaining green onions, bacon and cheese.

Yield: 8 servings

"One, if by land, and two, if by sea..."

So goes the poem written by Henry Wadsworth Longfellow and learned by every child in elementary school. The signal to Paul Revere came from the belfry atop theOld North Church in Boston. On April 18, 1775, the church sexton, Robert Newman, climbed the steeple and hung two lanterns thus beginning the War for Independence. After he lit the lanterns, he returned to ground level and crawled out a window. On the 200th anniversary of this momentous occasion, President Gerald Ford lit a third lantern that now hangs in this window. This new lantern is a symbol of freedom and resolve for the future.

Hungarian Mushroom Soup

12 ounces mushrooms, sliced
2 cups onions, chopped
2 tablespoons butter
3 tablespoons flour
1 cup skim milk
2 teaspoons dill weed
1 tablespoon Hungarian paprika
1 tablespoon tamari soy sauce
1 teaspoon salt
2 cups stock
2 teaspoons fresh lemon juice
¼ cup parsley, chopped
Fresh ground black pepper to taste
½ cup sour cream

1. Sauté onions and mushrooms in butter; salt lightly. Let cook until soft and onions are translucent. Add 1 teaspoons dill weed, ½ cup stock or water, tamari and paprika. Cover and simmer 15 minutes.
2. Melt 2 tablespoons butter in large saucepan. Whisk in flour and cook a few minutes, while continuing to whisk. Gradually add milk. Cook, stirring frequently, over low heat about 10 minutes, until thick.
3. Stir in mushroom mixture and remaining stock. Cover and simmer 10 to 15 minutes.
4. Before serving, season to taste; add lemon juice, sour cream and a sprinkle of dill. Garnish with parsley.

Yield: 4 servings

Cream of Broccoli Soup

4 tablespoons butter
2 tablespoons minced onion
½ cup celery, sliced
1 medium potato, peeled and sliced
1 small bunch broccoli, rinsed, trimmed and cut into 1-inch slices
2 sprigs parsley
2 cups milk
4 cups chicken broth
3 tablespoons cornstarch
2 cups half & half cream
Salt and pepper

1. In large stock pot, melt butter; add onion, celery, potato and parsley. Cook over low heat, stirring often until tender.
2. Add broccoli, milk and chicken broth; bring to boil. Simmer 25 minutes until tender.
3. Remove from heat; put soup in batches into blender or food processor. Dissolve cornstarch in half & half and add to broccoli mixture. Season with salt and pepper to taste.
4. Place over hot—not boiling—water until ready to serve.

Yield: 6 to 8 servings

Cook's Note: If desired, add a dash of either curry or paprika for additional flavor.

French Onion Soup

3 medium onions, thinly sliced
2 tablespoons butter, melted
1 tablespoon flour
2 cups consommé
4 cups water
¼ cup milk, scalded
¼ pound Swiss cheese, grated
6 slices dried french bread
Salt and pepper to taste
2 tablespoons butter, melted

1. In a heavy stock pot, cook onions in butter until slightly browned. Sprinkle with flour and cook over low heat until golden. Never allow onions to become dark in color.
2. Add consommé and water; bring to boil, stirring constantly. Reduce heat and simmer pot for 20 minutes uncovered.
3. Add milk and seasoning and heat through. Pour into individual ovenproof soup bowls. Place french bread on top; sprinkle generously with cheese. Pour a little melted butter on top and place under hot broiler until brown and bubbly.

Yield: 4 to 6 servings

When is a Castle Not a Castle?

In the case of John Smith of Perth, Scotland, his castle was a wood shack with a cave and terrace landscaping known as Hermit's Cave. Some say Smith was an actor, others a peddler, but it was affairs of the heart that drove him to become a hermit. The story goes that Smith was recovering from a failed relationship in Scotland and was searching for solitude. In the mid-1860s, Smith arrived from Scotland to New York and after a brief stay, moved on to Boston. He eventually settled in Erving where he lived for many years and became somewhat of a celebrity, receiving thousands of visitors.

Hermit's Cave was recently refurbished and can be visited daily. The trail begins off Route 2 in Erving. It is a moderately strenuous two-mile hike to the castle, so get on those hiking boots, pack a lunch and take plenty of water.

Pumpkin Soup

¼ cup butter
1 small onion, finely chopped
¼ teaspoon ginger
¼ teaspoon nutmeg
3 cups chicken broth
1 (15-ounce) can pumpkin
1 cup light cream
1 ounce brandy
Salt and pepper

1. Melt butter in large saucepan. Sauté onion in butter until soft.
2. Add spices and broth, and bring to boil. Add pumpkin and bring pot to boil.
3. Lower heat and slowly add cream. Do not boil. When heated through, add brandy. Season to taste.
4. Pour into soup dishes, or for a more festive touch, serve soup in small hollowed-out pumpkins.

Yield: 6 to 8 servings

Fresh Tomato Bisque

2 pounds ripe tomatoes (about 6)
1 onion, sliced thin
1 tablespoon butter
1 bay leaf
1 tablespoon brown sugar
2 whole cloves
1 teaspoon salt
½ teaspoon black pepper
1 teaspoon chopped fresh basil
1 pint light cream
1 cup milk
6 large toasted butter croutons
2 tablespoons chopped chives

1. Skin, seed and chop tomatoes. Sauté onion in butter and add tomatoes.
2. Add bay leaf, sugar, cloves, salt, pepper and basil. Simmer, stirring occasionally, until tomatoes are thoroughly cooked, about 25 minutes.
3. Remove bay leaf and cloves and transfer mixture to blender to purée (or strain through a coarse sieve).
4. Add cream and milk and heat through. Serve topped with toasted butter croutons.

Yield: 8 servings

Strawberry Soup

3 cups water
1½ cups red wine
1 cup sugar
¼ teaspoon lemon juice
¼ teaspoon cinnamon
2 quarts strawberries, puréed
1 cup heavy cream
⅓ cup sour cream

1. Combine water, wine, sugar, lemon juice and cinnamon. Simmer uncovered for 15 minutes, stirring occasionally. Add strawberry purée and simmer for 10 minutes more, stirring frequently. Chill
2. Whip cream until just stiff; do not overwhip. Fold whipped cream and sour cream into chilled berry mixture and chill.
3. Serve chilled with a dollop of sour cream and strawberry slice.

Yield: 6 to 8 servings

Glacial Potholes

The glacial potholes in Shelburne Falls formed when stones trapped in cracks are thrown about in the fast moving current, drilling their way into the bottom of the Deerfield River. Over 50 glacial potholes are clustered in one of the largest known concentrations of these natural sculptures. The potholes range in size from six inches in diameter to the largest pothole on record – 39 feet across. It is truly a beautiful site and a geological wonder.

Lobster Stew

4 (1½ pound) lobsters
1 tablespoon salt
1 teaspoon sugar
1 pint clam juice
1 pint water
1 sprig parsley
1 stalk celery, chopped coarsely
1 carrot, chopped coarsely
1 bay leaf
1 onion, studded with 2 cloves
2 tablespoons butter
½ tablespoon flour
Salt and pepper to taste
⅛ teaspoon nutmeg
⅛ teaspoon cayenne pepper
½ cup dry sherry
2 pints cream
Melted butter
Common crackers

1. Boil lobster 15 minutes in salted water with sugar added; remove.
2. Leave lobster meat whole; cut tail in large chunks and set aside.
3. Simmer bodies in clam juice, water, parsley, celery, carrot, bay leaf and studded onion.
4. Sauté meat in butter at low heat; sprinkle lightly with flour, salt, pepper, nutmeg and cayenne pepper; add sherry.
5. Add 1 cup broth and then add the cream. Add more sherry if desired. Heat gently, do not allow to boil.
6. Serve with melted butter and common crackers.

Yield: 6 to 8 servings

Tales of a Wayside Inn
by Henry Wadsworth Longfellow

One Autumn night, in Sudbury town,
Across the meadow bare and brown,
The windows of the Wayside Inn
Gleamed red with fire light through the leaves
Of woodbine, hanging from the eaves
Their crimson curtains rent and thin.

As ancient is this hostelry
As any in the land may be,
Built in the old Colonial day
When men lived in a grander way,
With ampler hospitality;
A kind of old Hobgoblin Hall,
Now somewhat fallen to decay,
With weather-stains upon the ways,
And stairsways worn, and crazy doors,
And creaking and uneven floors,
And chimneys huge, and tiled and tall.

Lobster Bisque

1 quart clam broth or seafood broth
Pinch thyme
1 bay leaf
Pinch white pepper
4 ounces sherry
2 stalks celery, chopped
1 (1-pound) lobster, cooked, cleaned, meat chopped fine, set aside
1 carrot, chopped
1 small onion, chopped
⅓ pound butter
1 cup flour
1½ teaspoons paprika
1½ pints light cream, heated

1. Bring broth to a boil and then simmer with seasonings, vegetables and half the indicated sherry for approximately one hour.
2. In a heavy stock pot, melt butter with paprika. Add flour to make a roux and cook for 5 to 10 minutes.
3. Strain stock into the roux and stir thoroughly. Allow to cook for another 10 to 15 minutes, whisking as necessary.
4. Add remaining sherry and lobster meat. Add hot light cream to finish. Heat through.

Source: Wayside Inn
Sudbury

Swan Boats and Daffodils Signal Spring

To most Bostonians, spring arrives when the daffodils and Swan Boats return to the Boston Public Gardens. For over 120 years, the Swan Boats have glided across the lagoon and under the world's smallest suspension bridge. In 1877, Roger Paget was granted a license to operate a boat-for-hire by the City of Boston. It was his idea to move the boats using a paddle wheel and turning it by having the driver sit in the back behind the swan design and use his legs as if he were riding a bicycle. Through three generations, the boats have gotten larger, but the designs remains unchanged.

Mariner's Fish Stew

4 slices bacon, diced
1 cup hot water
4 medium onions, quartered
1 (9-ounce) package frozen green beans
1½ teaspoons salt
½ teaspoon rosemary
¼ teaspoon thyme
2 pounds haddock or cod fillets
2 cups carrots, cooked
2 cans cream of potato soup
1 cup half & half cream
1 cup milk

1. Cook bacon. Place on paper toweling to drain.
2. In a 5-quart stockpot or dutch oven, add water, onions, green beans, rosemary and thyme. Cover and simmer for 10 minutes.
3. Add fish and continue to simmer for another 15 minutes. Add cooked carrots and potato soup; heat through.
4. Add milk and half & half; heat thoroughly, but do not allow to boil.

Yield: 8 servings

The Sounds of Music

Each year over 300,000 music lovers enjoy the summer home of the Boston Symphony high in the rolling hills of the Berkshires in the town of Lenox. Better known as the Tanglewood Music Center, many wonderful evenings are spent listening not only to the Symphony, but also the Boston Pops Orchestra and many great performers such as James Taylor and the late John Denver. It was and is a joy to listen to music conducted by such legends as Arthur Fiedler, Leonard Bernstein, John Williams, Suji Ozawa and Keith Lockhart.

Tanglewood Salad

3 ounces smoked ham
3 ounces turkey
4 ounces provolone
1 (9-ounce) package frozen green beans, thawed
8-10 cherry tomatoes, halved
1 cup pitted ripe olives, cut in half
4 whole hot cherry peppers

Dressing:
3 tablespoons red wine vinegar
½ teaspoon oregano
¼ teaspoon salt
Pinch of freshly ground pepper
1 clove garlic
3 tablespoons salad oil
3 tablespoons olive oil

1. Julienne ham, turkey and provolone. Place salad ingredients in a bowl and mix.
2. In a jar with a lid, combine and shake dressing ingredients until well combined. Cover and marinate for 2 hours or more. Pour over salad before serving.

Yield: 4 servings

Organic Gardening

Undoubtedly, the first organic gardening in the new world was taught to the Pilgrims by Native Americans. Town Brook runs through the middle of Brewster Gardens in Plymouth. The Indians taught the Pilgrims to place a herring in each hill of corn for fertilizer. This organic fertilizer led to an abundant crop that they then served at the First Thanksgiving dinner. Today, the Gardens are a wonderful spot to rest after a day of touring. You enter the Gardens from behind either the Jenney Grist Mill (the first gristmill in America) or by the harbor. Be sure to visit the Pilgrim Maiden statue and the new sculpture dedicated to the many immigrants who have blessed these shores.

Lobster Salad Rolls

Most New Englanders prefer their lobster salad rolls made with lobster, celery and mayonnaise. They omit other seasonings, as they do not want anything to interfere with the favor of the lobster. However, your taste buds might enjoy trying other seasonings such as the curry powder or onions.

2 cups lobster meat, finely chopped
½ cup celery, finely chopped
Sprinkle of lemon juice
½ cup mayonnaise (approximate)
Salt and pepper to taste
Softened butter
Frankfurter rolls
Shredded lettuce

1. Combine lobster meat and celery and sprinkle lightly with lemon juice. Mix slightly; add enough mayonnaise to bind mixture; stir well. Add salt and pepper to taste and mix well.
2. If necessary, partially slice frankfurter rolls; butter the outside surface well. Heat griddle or heavy skillet and toast rolls slowly on both sides until golden. Put about 2 tablespoons shredded lettuce inside each toasted roll.
3. Spoon about ½ cup of the lobster salad into each roll. Serve immediately while roll is still warm. Do not let stand unrefrigerated.

Yield: 5 servings

Potato Salad

6-8 potatoes, sliced thin, cooked
½ cup onions, diced
¼ cup celery, diced
½ cup vinegar
1 tablespoon sugar
Olive oil (see note)
2 shakes freshly ground pepper
2 tablespoons chopped or snipped parsley

1. Heat vinegar and sugar until sugar is dissolved. Do not boil.
2. Meanwhile, combine onions and celery with the sliced potatoes.
3. Pour hot vinegar mixture over potato combination.
4. Mix so all ingredients are well coated.

Source: former Guenther and Handel's Deli
Springfield

Cook's Note:
Add only enough olive oil to make the sound of someone smacking their lips over something delicious.

Broccoli Salad

4 broccoli crowns
1 small red onion, finely chopped
½ pound bacon
½ cup sunflower seeds
½ cup golden raisins
½ cup Monterey Jack cheese, grated
1 cup mayonnaise

1. Separate the broccoli into small florets, and slice the tender part of the stems. Steam over boiling water, covered until the color brightens, about 3 minutes. Do not overcook. You want the broccoli crunchy.
2. Cook bacon and crumble.
3. Place broccoli, bacon, onion, seeds, raisins and cheese in bowl. Mix with mayonnaise.
4. Chill thoroughly before serving.

Yield: 8 servings

Cook's Notes:
I like to cook bacon in the microwave. Place on a paper plate and cover with paper toweling. Cook three minutes; drain, turn and cook the other side three minutes.

Feel free to mix and change ingredients. Use pine nuts or slivered almonds in place of sunflower seeds. I like to use dried cranberries; they add color to the dish, or use a ¼ cup of each. For cheeses, try grated Cheddar or a mixture.

Jumptown

Orange, or Jumptown as it is know to thousands of parachuting enthusiasts, is located north of the Quabbin Reservoir. Orange is also the birth place of skydiving and home to the first commercial sport parachute center in the United States. Since opening in 1959, the skies over Orange are filled with thousands of jumpers from April to Thanksgiving.

In 1962 Orange hosted the World Parachute Meet, an Olympics-type skydiving competition. This event brought jumpers from around the world to the Orange Airport. In 2002, the Massachusetts Sport Parachute Club held a 40th anniversary celebration in remembrance of the Meet.

German Potato Salad (Kartoffelsalat)

6 large potatoes
¼ pound bacon, diced
1 medium onion, chopped
¼ cup sugar
2 tablespoons flour
1 teaspoon salt
½ cup vinegar
½ cup water
Minced parsley

1. Cook potatoes, covered, in boiling salted water in a large saucepan until tender, about 40 minutes; drain. Cool until easy to handle, then slice about ¼-inch thick.
2. Sauté bacon until crisp; pour off drippings. Measure 2 tablespoons and return to pan. Stir onion into drippings and sauté until brown. Blend in sugar, flour and salt, then vinegar and water. Cook until mixture thickens and boils, about one minute.
3. Fold in potatoes and bacon carefully. Let stand in warm area 15 to 30 minutes to blend flavors. Sprinkle with parsley. Serve warm.

Yield: 6 servings

Roasted Beet Salad

4 medium beets
1 cup balsamic vinegar
½ cup sugar
⅛ cup olive oil
2 tablespoons sesame seeds
1 medium spanish or sweet onion
½ cup blue cheese, crumbled
6-8 cups lettuce and baby greens

1. Preheat oven to 375º.
2. Place beets in a 9x9-inch roasting pan and cover with aluminum foil. Place in oven and roast until tender, approximately 1 to 1½ hours.
3. In a non-reactive saucepan, place balsamic vinegar and sugar. Set on high heat and bring to a boil. Reduce heat to medium and allow mixture to reduce to half. When reduced, set aside.
4. Toast sesame seeds until golden. Either place in oven or in a dry sauté pan on top of stove. When golden, add to vinegar; whisk in oil.
5. When beets are tender, remove from oven and allow too cool. When cool, peel and slice.
6. Slice onion into half-moon slices. In a sauté, add sliced beets and onions. Add ½ cup of the balsamic salad dressing. Make sure the dressing is well blended. Sauté until beets and onions are warmed through. Onions still should be al dente. Dressing should be hot.
7. Place greens in a salad bowl. Pour in remaining dressing and toss. Greens should begin to wilt slightly. Arrange greens on individual plates. Top with beets and onions, and crumbled blue cheese.

Yield: 8 servings

Monomoy Island

Off the eastern seaboard of Cape Code near Chatham, lies a spit of land called Monomoy Island. It is a barrier island subject to the change of seasons, tides and, in some cases, man. The island was once inhabited by man. In 1711, there was a tavern for sailors at Wreck Cove near where Hospital Pond is today. In the mid-1800s, the fishing community of Whitewash Village was located near present Powder Hole.

At times Monomoy Island has been one long peninsula; at other times, two separate islands. In 1958, a severe winter storm created Monomoy Island by separating it from the mainland. Another storm 20 years later cut through the relatively new island. These changes, and an increasing water level, have caused many houses along the Chatham shoreline to fall into the water. Residents of Chatham have tried unsuccessfully for years to get the government to fill in the pass created by storms. Monomoy Island is now a wildlife refuge and home to plovers and other migratory birds.

Apple Coleslaw

¼ cup sour cream
¼ cup mayonnaise
½ teaspoon celery seed
1 teaspoon sugar
Dash of salt
1½ teaspoons lemon juice
2½ cups shredded cabbage
1 apple, unpeeled and sliced

1. Combine sour cream, mayonnaise, celery seed, sugar, salt and lemon juice in a small bowl; stir well.
2. Combine cabbage and apple in a large bowl, tossing lightly. Pour salad dressing over cabbage mixture; toss lightly to coat.

Yield: 4 to 6 servings

Mandarin Chicken Salad

2 pounds chicken breast, boned and skinned
2 cups celery, sliced
5 ounces slivered almonds
2 (11-ounce) cans mandarin oranges, drained
3 medium cantaloupes, halved, seeded and chilled
¾ cup sour cream
¾ cup mayonnaise
2 tablespoons lemon juice
2 tablespoons fresh ginger, grated
1 tablespoon fresh orange peel, grated
½ teaspoon salt
Dash nutmeg

1. Cook chicken breast (roast, bake or grill) and cube.
2. In a large bowl, combine chicken, celery, almonds and oranges.
3. In a small bowl, blend together sour cream, mayonnaise, lemon juice, ginger, orange peel, salt and nutmeg. Add just enough dressing to chicken mixture to bind.
4. Chill and serve in cantaloupe halves. Garnish wish sliced on cantaloupe and other melons.

Yield: 6 servings

Red Cabbage Slaw

½ head red cabbage, finely shredded
¾ cup raisins
¾ cup grated apple
¼ cup lowfat mayonnaise
2 teaspoons horseradish
¼ teaspoon salt
¼ cup plain yogurt

1. Mix cabbage, apple and raisins in a salad bowl.
2. In a small bowl, combine horseradish, salt, mayonnaise and yogurt. Stir into cabbage mixture carefully. Chill.

Yield: 4 servings

A House Made of Paper, Impossible!

Not so! In 1922, Elis Stenman, inventor of the machine that make paperclips, built a house in Rockport. Instead of clapboards on the side of the house, he began to layer the house with paper. He applied glue and then covered the layer with varnish. The result was a thick layer of compressed paper. Not only is the outside of the home made of paper, but also the inside and the furniture. The house is really quite amazing – 80 years later, the house is still standing. The exterior is re-varnished quite frequently so it remains waterproof. A little imagination and a lot of creativity have created one of the more unusual houses in Massachusetts.

Pineapple Pasta Primavera

1 can pineapple chunks
3 cups cooked spiral pasta
¼ cup chopped cilantro or parsley
½ cup reduced-calorie Italian salad dressing
2 cups snow peas
1 cup sliced carrots
1 cup sliced cucumbers
½ cup sliced radishes

1. Drain pineapple; reserve ¼ cup of juice.
2. Combine pineapple, reserved juice, pasta and vegetables in large bowl.
3. Toss to coat.

Yield: 6 to 8 servings

Chef's Note:
It is best to make this salad several hours or even a day ahead of serving so the spices and fruits can enhance the flavor.

Spinach and Bacon Salad with Warm Bacon Dressing

4 Red Delicious apples, cored, but not peeled
8 cups spinach, washed and torn
2 cups mushrooms, sliced
8 thin slices red onion
12 slices bacon
1 tablespoon Dijon mustard
2 tablespoons balsamic vinegar
3 tablespoons honey

1. Mix apples, spinach, mushrooms, and red onions together.
2. In heavy fry pan, stir and fry bacon over medium heat. When crisp, remove bacon to drain on paper plates or towels. Pour off all but two tablespoons fat. With wire whip, mix in mustard, vinegar and honey; blend until smooth. Season with salt and pepper.
3. Toss salad with warm bacon dressing and scatter bacon on top. Serve immediately.

Yield: 4 servings

Warm Bacon Dressing

12 slices bacon
1 tablespoon Dijon mustard
2 tablespoons balsamic vinegar
3 tablespoons honey

1. In a heavy fry pan, stir and fry bacon over medium heat. When crisp, remove and drain on paper plates or paper toweling.
2. Pour off all but 2 tablespoons of fat. With wire whip, mix in mustard, vinegar and honey; blend until smooth. Season with salt and pepper. Pour over salad greens immediately.

Frozen Peach and Pecan Salad

8 peach halves
1 cup cream, whipped
1 cup pecans, chopped
1 cup mayonnaise
1 cup cream cheese

1. Mix cream cheese, mayonnaise, whipped cream and pecans together.
2. Pour mixture over peaches, which have been placed, hollow side up, in tray of ice box.
3. Freeze 3 or 4 hours.
4. Serve on crisp lettuce.

Bash Bish Falls

Whether it is referred to Bish Bash or Bash Bish Falls State Park, visitors will find not only spectacular scenery, but also the highest single drop waterfall in southeastern New England. Located in the town of Mount Washington in the Berkshires, a brook cuts a 1,000 foot deep path through a narrow gorge of straight-walled cliffs before tumbling eighty feet into a crystal clear pool. The brook then flows through New York state until it meets the Hudson River.

Chatham Fruit Salad

1 (16-ounce) can cling peaches
1 (16-ounce) can pears
2 (8-ounce) cans chunk pineapple
1 (6-ounce) jar cherries, chopped
3 bananas, sliced
¾ can cranberry sauce

Dressing:
½ pint heavy cream
½ cup mayonnaise
¾ cup confectioners sugar
1½ teaspoons vanilla

1. Whip cranberry sauce with mixer and set aside.
2. Drain all fruit.
3. Combine fruits in a container that can be covered.
4. Pour dressing over fruit, cover and chill overnight.
5. Add bananas just before serving.
6. For dressing, whip cream until soft and creamy.
7. Stir in mayonnaise.
8. Fold in confectioners sugar and vanilla, and beat.

Yield: 6 servings

Cucumber, Tomato and Onion Salad

2 large ripe tomatoes
2 cucumbers
1 Vidalia or Bermuda onion
½ cup Greek Kalamata olives
½ cup olive oil
¼ cup lemon juice
½ teaspoon fresh oregano
2 teaspoons minced fresh basil or 1 teaspoon dry
Season to taste

1. Cut tomatoes in half lengthwise and slice; peel and slice cucumbers; and peel, slice and separate onion into rings.
2. Arrange vegetables on a serving plate, alternating vegetables. Sprinkle olives over top.
3. Combine oil, lemon juice, oregano and basil. Pour over vegetables. Add salt and pepper to taste. Chill before serving.

Yield: 4 to 6 servings

Belgian Endive Salad

1 pound Belgian endive
4 tablespoons Gorgonzola cheese
6 tablespoons plain yogurt
2 tablespoons brandy
Pinch of cayenne pepper

1. Trim, wash and dry endive leaves. Slice in half lengthwise and arrange on salad plates.
2. In small bowl, using a fork, mash cheese and yogurt well; add brandy and cayenne pepper.
3. To serve, spoon dressing over endive leaves.

Yield: 4 servings

Frozen Cranberry Salad

1 can cranberry jelly
½ pint heavy cream, whipped
2-3 tablespoons lemon juice
3 ounces softened cream cheese
½ cup mayonnaise
½ cup confectioners sugar

1. Combine cranberry jelly and whipped cream in bowl and freeze.
2. Combine remainder of ingredients; spread on top of frozen mixture. Return to freezer. When ready to serve, invert bowl and let salad slide out.

Yield: 8 servings

Cook's Note: This salad is very tasty with fowl and roast beef.

The Pots Begin to Boil...It Must Be Spring!

From mid-February until early April as the days begin to warm and the nights drop to freezing temperatures, the sap begins to run in sugar maples across New England and the pots begin to boil. This is a sure sign that spring is on its way. Sugarhouses that have been dormant for months open their doors on weekends for wonderful breakfasts where vast quantities of maple syrup are poured over pancakes, french toast and waffles.

Not all maple trees produce sap. Only the sugar maple (acer saccharum) is indigenous to the northeastern parts of the United States and Canada. The sugar maple can be tapped when a tree reaches 40 years of age and it will continue producing sap for another 60 years. It takes approximately 40 gallons of sap to make just one gallon of maple syrup. This is why maple syrup is often referred to as "liquid gold."

Strawberry Spinach Salad

1 (12-ounce) package fresh spinach
1 quart strawberries, stemmed and halved
1 cup pine nuts
½ cup vegetable oil
¼ cup cider vinegar
¼ teaspoon Dijon mustard
¼ cup sugar
1 small onion, grated
Salt and pepper to taste
2 teaspoons poppy seeds

1. Wash and drain spinach. In a serving bowl, tear spinach into bite-size pieces. Add strawberries and pine nuts.
2. For dressing, blend together all ingredients except poppy seeds. Process until smooth. Stir in poppy seeds.
3. Toss dressing with salad and serve immediately.

Yield: 6 servings

Coleslaw

1 medium head cabbage
¼ pound golden raisins
1 large garlic clove
8 ounces sour cream
2 tablespoons sugar
2 tablespoons cider vinegar
1 teaspoon curry powder (optional)
Salt and pepper to taste

1. Remove the outer leaves from the cabbage. Trim, quarter and core cabbage. Cut each quarter into ¼-inch shreds.
2. Place cabbage in a large bowl, add raisins and mix.
3. Mince garlic clove and place in small bowl. Add sour cream, sugar, vinegar, curry, salt and pepper and mix until smooth.
4. Pour sour cream dressing over the cabbage-raisin mixture and toss to coat. Let coleslaw stand at room temperature for 30 minutes to marinate.
5. Refrigerate until ready to serve.

Yield: 8 to 10 servings

Green Bean Salad

2 cups cooked, cut green beans
2 cups lettuce, shredded
2 whole green onions, chopped
2 sprigs summer savory, minced
Salt and pepper to taste

1. Mix cold, cooked green beans with shredded lettuce.
2. Sprinkle green onion over salad. Add herbs and seasonings.
3. Decorate with seasonal blossoms such as pansies or nasturtiums.
4. Serve with vinaigrette or dressing of choice.

Yield: 8 servings

The Raid on Deerfield

Three hundred years ago in the early dawn of a cold winter day, over 200 French and Indian troops attacked the village of Deerfield. The raiding party killed many, burned the village and took captives. The prisoners were forced to walk to Canada, with many dying or being killed along the way. Upon reaching Canada, the prisoners were divided between the Indians and French. Some were redeemed, either purchased or exchanged for prisoners held by the British; others remained with their captors. It is believed that between three and five percent of today's French Canadian population is descended from these English captives.

Tabouli

1 cup cracked bulger
Boiling water
1 pound tomatoes, peeled, seeded and chopped
2 cups green onion, chopped
3 cups fresh parsley, chopped
2 tablespoons fresh mint
⅓ cup olive oil
⅓ cup fresh lemon juice
1 teaspoon salt
½ teaspoon ground pepper

1. Rinse bulger; cover with boiling water and let stand for 30 minutes. Drain thoroughly and squeeze dry using either cheesecloth or a linen towel.
2. Combine tomatoes, green onion, parsley and mint in a large salad bowl.
3. Beat together oil, lemon juice, salt and pepper. Fold into tomato mixture.
4. Mix in bulger until well-blended.
5. Cover and chill before serving.

Yield: 6 to 8 servings

Entrees

Newburyport

Cape Cod National Seashore

In 1961, the federal government purchased land that makes up the Cape Cod National Seashore Park. This was the first time that government monies were used to establish a national park. The park stretches from Chatham to Race Point in Provincetown. For once some of the glorious beaches and dunes won out over condos and development, and our tax dollars were put to good use.

Chicken and Yellow Rice (Arroz con Pollo)

1 (10-ounce) package uncooked rice with saffron
1 medium green pepper, seeded and diced
1 small tomato sauce
2 teaspoons salt
1 bay leaf
6 chicken breasts
1 large onion, chopped
2 cloves garlic minced
1 can condensed chicken broth
1 cup water
1 (10-ounce) package frozen peas

1. Preheat oven to 350°.
2. Mix rice, green peppers, tomatoes, salt and bay leaf in an 8x13-inch oven-to-table casserole dish.
3. Brown chicken in olive oil over medium heat, place on top of rice mixture.
4. Stir onion and garlic into drippings in pan. Sauté until soft. Stir in chicken broth and water; heat to boiling. Pour over chicken. Cover casserole with aluminum foil.
5. Bake one hour or until chicken and rice are tender, and liquid is absorbed. Heat peas thoroughly and spoon around edge of chicken casserole. Serve hot.

Yield: 6 servings

Chicken Breast with Prosciutto and Marsala

2 ounces dried porcini mushrooms
4 chicken breasts, skinned and boned
Flour seasoned with salt and pepper
3 tablespoons olive oil
4 tablespoons butter
½ pound fresh mushrooms, quartered
½ cup Marsala wine
4 ounces prosciutto, julienne

1. Combine porcini mushrooms in a small bowl with enough warm water to cover. Let sit about 30 minutes to soften.
2. Drain mushrooms in a strainer lined with dampened paper towels. Rinse mushrooms with cold water to remove any lingering dirt or sand. Remove mushrooms from liquid, reserving liquid, pat dry and chop coarsely.
3. Preheat oven to 250º.
4. Dredge chicken lightly in seasoned flour. In a large skillet, heat olive oil and butter over medium-high heat. Sauté chicken breast until lightly browned on both sides. Transfer chicken to plate and keep warm in oven.
5. Add porcini and fresh mushroom to skillet and sauté over medium-high heat, stirring frequently for 5 minutes. Pour in Marsala wine and ½ cup of reserved mushroom liquid. Bring to boil; reduce heat and simmer until sauce has thickened.
6. Add prosciutto and chicken to skillet (along with any juices on plate). Cover and simmer the mixture for 15 minutes or until chicken is cooked through.
7. Divide chicken on flour plates and spoon the prosciutto and mushroom sauce over the chicken. Serve immediately.

Yield: 4 servings

Tulips and Daffodils

In the spring, the Boston Public Gardens come alive with tulips and daffodils. Established in 1837, the gardens are the first public botanical garden in the United States. George V. Meacham, winner of a design competition and one hundred dollars, designed the original 24-acre gardens. The Public Gardens are the home to Boston's famous swan boats, the world's shortest suspension bridge, and the brass replicas of the feathered friends from *Make Way for Ducklings* by Robert McColsky.

Chicken Breast Piquant

2 chicken breasts, halved, skinned and boned
1 (8-ounce) can crushed pineapple
1 (6-ounce) can frozen limeade, thawed
1½ ounces light rum
3 whole cloves
⅓ cup all-purpose flour
2 teaspoons salt
4 tablespoons butter
⅓ cup slivered almonds

1. With a meat mallet, pound chicken until ½-inch thick.
2. Mix together pineapple and juices, limeade, light rum and cloves in shallow container with cover. Add chicken, turning to coat. Cover and marinate chicken at room temperature for 30 minutes. Remove the chicken and reserve marinade.
3. Mix flour and salt. Add chicken, coating all sides.
4. Sauté chicken in melted butter until all sides are golden brown, about 10 minutes.
5. Place chicken in greased baking dish; pour reserved marinade over; and sprinkle top with slivered almonds.
6. Preheat oven to 400°. Bake uncovered, basting twice, for about 25 minutes or until fork-tender.
7. Place chicken on serving plate and pour marinade over.

Yield: 4 servings

Chicken Cacciatore

2 pounds chicken breasts or tenders
¼ cup flour
¼ cup cooking oil
2 medium onions, coarsely chopped
2 medium green peppers, chopped
1 garlic clove, minced
1¼ teaspoons salt
Dash pepper
2 bay leaves
1 (16-ounce) can tomatoes
1 (8-ounce) can tomato sauce
¼ cup dry white wine

1. Preheat electric skillet to 350º.
2. Cut chicken in large pieces and coat with flour. Heat oil in pan; add chicken and cook until lightly browned, turning as needed. Remove chicken.
3. Add onions, green peppers and garlic and cook about 3 minutes. Add seasonings, tomatoes, tomato sauce and wine.
4. Cover, reduce heat to simmer and cook 30 minutes or until chicken is tender. Turn chicken occasionally.

Yield: 6 to 8 servings

Chicken Breasts in Wine Sauce

8 chicken breasts, boned
Chopped parsley
Garlic butter
Flour
1 egg, beaten with
1 tablespoon water
Breadcrumbs
½ cup almonds
1½ cups chicken broth
1 chicken bouillon cube
½ cup sherry wine
1 teaspoon tarragon
Salt and pepper to taste

1. Preheat oven to 300°.
2. Flatten chicken. Spread with garlic butter and chopped parsley. Roll the stuffed chicken. Roll in flour, dip in egg and roll in breadcrumbs.
3. Brown chicken rolls in skillet in small amount of butter or margarine. Be careful not to burn. Place in 9x13-inch pan after browned.
4. To make sauce, sauté almonds in drippings, add broth and 1 scant tablespoon flour, bouillon cube, sherry, tarragon, salt and pepper; mix well. Pour sauce over chicken rolls.
5. Bake uncovered for 1 hour.

The Midnight Ride of Paul Revere

"Listen my children, and you shall hear, Of the midnight ride of Paul Revere...." "One, if by land, and two, if by sea; And I on the opposite shore will be, Ready to ride and spread the alarm through every Middlesex village and farm..."

Henry Wadsworth Longfellow, 1860

Paul Revere (1734-1818) was first and foremost a silversmith, but he was also a patriot and an industrialist. In 1860, he became a legend after the poem, "Paul Revere's Ride" by Henry Wadsworth Longfellow, was published. In 1801, Revere opened the first copper rolling mill in North America. His firm supplied copper for the hull of the USS Constitution and the new State House dome. Today Revere Copper and Brass is best known for its Revereware® copper-bottom pans.

Sweet and Sour Chicken

1 pound boneless chicken, cubed
2 tablespoon olive oil
1 garlic clove, minced
1 large green pepper, julienne
2 large carrots, julienne
1½ cups chicken broth
¼ cup soy sauce
2 tablespoons sherry
3 tablespoons brown sugar
½ teaspoon ginger
1 (8-ounce) can pineapple chunks
1½ cups Minute® rice

1. Brown chicken in olive oil.
2. Add garlic, pepper and carrots; sauté briefly. Add chicken broth, soy sauce, cherry, brown sugar, ginger and pineapple with juice. Bring to a full boil.
3. Add rice and stir; cover and let stand 5 minutes. Stir before serving.

Yield: 4 servings

Peach Brandy Chicken

4 boneless skinless chicken breasts
½ cup milk
1 tablespoon butter
2 tablespoons flour
4 small peaches or canned peaches
Salt and pepper, pinch
Dried tarragon, or a sprig of fresh
3 ounces peach brandy
⅓ cup chicken stock

1. Heat butter in sauté pan. Dip chicken in milk and then in flour, and sauté over medium-high heat until brown (about 4 to 5 minutes). Turn breasts and cook another 4 to 5 minutes. Thinner breasts or chicken tenders will require less time.

2. Remove breasts from pan and deglaze pan with chicken stock. Add peaches, brandy and tarragon; reduce heat and cook approximately 2 minutes.

3. Return chicken, along with accumulated juices, to pan. Cook until chicken is hot and cook through.

Cook's Note:
If sauce is not quite thick enough after removing chicken, reduce quickly on high heat before pouring over chicken.

Apricot Chicken Breast

1 cup diced dried apricots
1 cup apple juice or cider
2 boneless skinless chicken breasts, halved
Salt
Paprika, preferably Hungarian
1 tablespoon oil
1 tablespoon butter
3 tablespoon chopped shallots
¼ cup dry vermouth
¼ teaspoon mace
½ cup chopped toasted almonds

1. Soak apricots in apple juice or cider.

2. Sprinkle chicken with salt to taste and paprika. Heat oil and butter over heat in large skillet. Add shallots; sauté about 2 minutes. Add chicken; cook until lightly browned, 2 to 3 minutes per side.

3. Drain apricots reserving ½ cup apple juice. Add the juice, vermouth and mace to skillet. Reduce heat to low; simmer covered about 10 minutes. Stir in apricots; simmer covered 5 minutes longer.

4. Sprinkle with almonds. Serve with rice or pilaf.

Yield: 4 servings

The County Fair

The county fair is as much a part of Massachusetts' heritage as the town meeting. Massachusetts has many small fairs, but the Topsfield Fair and the Eastern States Exposition (better known as the Big E) in West Springfield are among the oldest and largest.

The Topsfield Fair is America's oldest agricultural fair. Begun in 1818, it has been held every year with the exception of six times. By government decree, the fair was suspended for three years during the Civil War and for three years during World War II (1943-1945).

The Big E is the largest fair in the Northeast with over one million attendees annually. A replica of each state capitol building represents the six New England states. Visitors can sample both the architectural style and the traditional foods and wares that exemplify each state.

Massachusetts is a state known for its high-tech and biotech industries, but agriculture plays a large role too and we need to remember those roots and protect the farms and lands from development.

Apricot-Glazed Chicken in Wine

1 (17-ounce) can apricot halves, drained
1 tablespoon lemon juice
12 chicken breast halves, boned, skinned
1 stick butter, melted
1 cup white wine
2 tablespoons oregano
2 teaspoons garlic salt

1. Drain apricots and puree halves in blender. Blend apricot puree with lemon juice, melted butter, wine, oregano, and garlic salt.
2. Place chicken in 9x13-inch pan in a single layer. Pour apricot mixture over chicken.
3. Bake at 325° for one hour, basting chicken occasionally. Serve with wild rice or pilaf.

Yield: 6 to 8 servings

Chicken Tetrazzini

The first time I had this entree was many years ago in Easthampton, NY at a birthday party for a donkey named Esmerelda. She wasn't just any ole donkey, but one that was much loved. It was quite a birthday party and the guest of honor was festooned in a daisy chain necklace and crown.

½ pound angel hair spaghetti
1 pound fresh mushrooms, sliced
3 cups chicken, cut in strips
½ cup almonds, blanched, slivered
¼ cup parsley, chopped
3 tablespoons butter
2 tablespoons flour
2 cups chicken broth
Salt and pepper to taste
1 cup heavy cream
¼ dry white wine
Grated Parmesan cheese

1. Boil spaghetti. Spray a nonstick pan with oil and sauté mushrooms. Combine spaghetti and mushrooms in a large bowl.
2. Place chicken, almonds and parsley in second bowl.
3. Make the sauce by melting the butter; stir in flour and cook the mixture for 2 to 3 minutes making a roux. Gradually add broth and seasonings and cook slowly until mixture is quite thick. Remove from heat and slowly add cream and wine.
4. Divide sauce equally between the two bowls. Butter a large casserole dish (wider is better) and place spaghetti and mushrooms in the dish. Layer contents of second bowl over spaghetti. Sprinkle with freshly grated Parmesan cheese over the top.
5. Bake in a preheated oven at 350° for 30 to 40 minutes until top is bubbly and golden.

Cook's Note:
This recipe takes substitutions very well. If you don't like nuts, remove them; if you like green beans, add them. For a less fattening dish, use half & half with a little more flour to thicken the sauce.

Cradle of Liberty

"The City of Boston, the Cradle of Liberty, may Faneuil Hall ever stand a monument to teach the world that resistance to oppression is a duty, and will, under true republican institutions become a blessing."

General Lafayette, 1825

Constructed in 1740, Faneuil Hall earned its nickname, Cradle of Liberty, because it was used as a meeting place for American patriots before and during the Revolutionary War. In 1805, American architect Charles Bulfinch designed an addition to Faneuil Hall that allowed it to hold up to 1,000 people. Today, it is the cornerstone of Quincy Market and is still in use as a museum and meeting hall.

Champagne Chicken

2 tablespoons all-purpose flour
1 teaspoon salt
¼ teaspoon pepper
4 skinned and boned chicken breast halves
2 tablespoons butter
1 tablespoon olive oil
1 cup champagne or dry white wine
½ cup sliced fresh mushrooms
½ cup whipping cream

1. Combine flour, salt and pepper in a shallow dish. Dredge chicken in flour mixture.
2. Heat butter and oil in a large skillet; add chicken, and sauté for 3 to 4 minutes on each side. Add champagne or wine, cook over medium heat about 12 minutes or until chicken is done.
3. Remove chicken and set aside. Add mushrooms to skillet and sauté for 1 to 2 minutes. Add whipping cream to skillet; cover over medium heat, stirring constantly, just until thickened.
4. Add chicken, and cook until thoroughly heated. Serve warm.

Yield: 4 servings

Chicken Pot Pie

4 whole chicken breasts
1½ quarts water
¼ cup white wine
½ teaspoon dried rosemary
1 clove garlic, crushed
2 small bay leaves
½ teaspoon leaf thyme
¼ teaspoon leaf tarragon
4 whole black peppercorns
¼ cup clarified butter
¼ cup flour
2 carrots, peeled and diced
24 pearl onions
1 cup frozen peas
¼ cup white wine
6 buttermilk biscuits

1. Butter six individual crocks or ramekins.
2. Combine chicken, water, wine, herbs and peppercorns in a large pot. Bring to a boil over high heat, skimming off any foam that rises to the surface. Reduce heat and simmer for 20 to 30 minutes, or until chicken is tender. Remove chicken from the pot, and let it cool slightly. Remove skin, and separate meat from bones. Set meat aside and keep warm.
3. Return chicken to stock, and simmer until the stock has reduced by half, about 15 minutes. Strain stock and bring it back to a boil.
4. Over low heat, melt clarified butter in a small saucepan. Stir in flour, and bring roux to a slow boil. Cook without browning for 5 minutes. Add this roux to the stock, and simmer for another 10 minutes. Check for taste and adjust seasonings as desired. Keep the sauce warm.
5. In separate saucepans, cook carrots and pearl onions in boiling salted water to cover until just tender, about 8 to 10 minutes for carrots and 12 to 13 minutes for onions.
6. Dice chicken, and toss it with peas, cooked onions and carrots. Divide mixture among six individual crocks or ramekins. Pour sauce over chicken, and top with a biscuit. Serve piping hot.

Yield: 6 servings

Source: Red Lion Inn
Stockbridge

Lizzie Borden Had an Ax

The house at 92 Second Street in Fall River is now the Lizzie Borden Bed & Breakfast, but over 100 years ago, it was the scene of one of the most dastardly and diabolical crimes that was ever committed in Massachusetts. According to the folk song, "Lizzie Borden had an ax, and gave her mother forty whacks. And when she saw what she had done, she gave her father forty-one." Though everyone believed Lizzie murdered her parents, she was found not guilty and lived out the remainder of her life in Fall River.

Chicken Normandy

6 chicken breasts with skin
⅓ cup butter
½ cup apple juice
½ cup vermouth, very dry sherry or white wine
2 onions, sliced
½ cup heavy cream
Salt and pepper to taste
3 apples, sliced or cut

1. Preheat oven to 350°.
2. Sauté the chicken pieces in butter. Remove them as they brown, and add the onions till they yellow. Place the chicken and onions in a shallow baking dish, and pour the apple juice and the wine into the frying pan.
3. Over a medium flame, scrape up all the brown bits that have adhered to the pan. When the liquid has cooked down a bit, add the cream, salt and pepper, and continue cooking slowly for about 5 minutes.
4. Pour this sauce over the chicken and onions, add the cut apples and bake, covered for about twenty minutes. (Use aluminum foil if pan has no cover.)
5. Remove the cover and bake uncovered for another 10 minutes. The liquid should be saucy but not soupy; add more of the liquids judiciously during the baking process, if needed, and baste occasionally. Serve in the baking dish, along with very fine noodles.

Yield: 6 servings

Lemon Veal

2 tablespoons flour
2 teaspoons beef-flavored bouillon
½ teaspoon paprika
½ teaspoon chopped fresh parsley
¼ teaspoon dried rosemary
⅛ teaspoon pepper
1 pound boneless round rump veal, trimmed and cut into 1-inch cubes
4 medium carrots, cut into thin strips
½ cup dry white wine
½ cup water
2 tablespoons lemon juice

1. Combine flour, bouillon, paprika, parsley, rosemary and pepper in a plastic bag. Place veal in bag and shake until well-coated.
2. Spray pan with cooking oil. Place over medium heat until hot. Add veal and cook until lightly browned, stirring constantly.
3. Add carrots, white wine, water and lemon juice; bring to a boil, stirring constantly. Cover, reduce heat and simmer for 40 minutes.
4. Add veal, placing seam down and cook over medium-high heat
5. Serve with noodles or over rice.

Yield: 4 servings

Veal Cordon Bleu

1 pound veal leg round steak, cut ¼-inch thick
2 slices Swiss cheese
2 slices boiled ham
⅔ cup dry breadcrumbs
1 tablespoon snipped parsley
⅛ teaspoon pepper
¼ cup all-purpose flour
1 egg, slightly beaten
¼ cup butter or margarine

1. Cut veal into 4 pieces and pound with a meat mallet to ⅛-inch thickness. Cut each piece of veal in half crosswise.
2. Dice cheese and ham. Put a few pieces of both cheese and ham on top of slice of veal. Cover with a second piece of veal and seal edges. Repeat with the remaining veal.
3. Combine breadcrumbs, parsley and pepper. Dip veal in flour, egg and crumb mixture (in that order).
4. In a skillet, melt butter or margarine. Add veal and cook over medium-high heat for about 4 minutes per side or until golden.

Is It Spelled Correctly?

In 1806, Noah Webster published the first American dictionary, *A Compendious Dictionary of the English Language.* In 1831, Charles and George Merriam opened a printing company and bookselling operation in Springfield. After Webster's death, the Merriam brothers secured the rights to his 1841 edition of *An American Dictionary of the English Language, Corrected and Enlarged.* This was beginning of a publishing tradition that has continued to this day as Merriam-Webster.

Veal with Bacon and Vermouth Sauce

3 strips of bacon, chopped
1 pound potatoes, peeled
1¾ pounds veal scallops
½ cup all purpose flour
2 tablespoons butter
1 cup chicken broth
⅓ cup dry vermouth
2 garlic cloves, minced
2 teaspoons fresh thyme, chopped

1. Chop peeled potatoes into ½-inch cubes.
2. Cook bacon in large nonstick skillet. Remove bacon to small bowl.
3. Add potatoes to dripping in skillet. Cover and cook until potatoes are tender, about 10 minutes. Stir occasionally. Transfer potatoes to medium bowl. Either cover to keep warm or put in warming oven.
4. Sprinkle veal with salt and pepper; coat with four and shake off excess. Add butter to skillet and melt over medium-high heat. Working in batches, add veal to skillet and cook until brown, about 2 minutes per side. Transfer veal to warm platter.
5. Add broth, vermouth, garlic and thyme to skillet and bring to boil, making sure you scrap up any browned bits. Boil until sauce is reduced to ¾ cup. Mix in bacon. Season with salt and pepper. Pour sauce over veal. Surround with potatoes.

Yield: 4 servings

Osso Buco Milanese

3 meaty veal shanks,
cut into 2-inch pieces
½ cup flour, seasoned with
salt and pepper
2 tablespoons olive oil
2 tablespoons butter
½ cup chopped onion
¼ cup chopped celery
¼ cup chopped carrot
¼ teaspoon rosemary
½ cup dry white wine or vermouth
2 tablespoons tomato paste
½ cup water
1 lemon, grated rind
2 tablespoons finely chopped parsley
1 garlic clove, minced

1. Roll veal shanks in flour. In large heavy saucepan, over brisk heat, brown shanks on all sides in hot oil and butter, for about 10 minutes.
2. Add onions, carrots, celery and rosemary. Continue cooking until shanks are well browned and vegetables are soft and begin to take on color.
3. Arrange cuts on their meatiest sides to hold in the marrow. Add the wine and cook until it evaporates. Mix together the tomato paste and water and add to pan.
4. Lower heat and cook covered for two hours or until meat is fork tender; add liquid as necessary.
5. Place shanks on a hot platter. Bring pan juices to a boil, scrapping bottom; add liquid as needed. Mix lemon rind, parsley and garlic. Add half to the sauce. Cook 5 minutes longer. Pour sauce over meat and garnish with remaining lemon rind mix.

Yield: 4 to 6 servings

Source: Frigo's Restaurant
Springfield

Poets Seat Tower

Atop a hill in the Western Massachusetts town of Greenfield, is a stone tower erected in 1912 at the site where Frederick Goddard Tuckerman was inspired to write poetry. The climb is three-stories to the top, but it's well worth it with spectacular views of the Pioneer Valley awaiting those who persevere. The Tower is also a great spot to watch the annual migrations of birds.

Veal Marsala

⅓ cup onions, finely diced
½ pound shiitake mushrooms, sliced ¼-inch
1 pound veal scallops, pounded thin
½ cup flour
2 tablespoons oil
5 tablespoons butter or margarine
¾ cup chicken broth
⅔ cup Marsala wine
⅓ cup fresh parsley, chopped
Salt and pepper to taste

1. Preheat sauté pan on medium-high for 2 to 3 minutes. Place 1 tablespoon butter in pan and swirl to coat. Add onions, stir and cook for 2 minutes.
2. Add remaining butter and mushrooms; continue to cook for another 3 minutes; remove onion and mushrooms to warm dish.
3. Dust veal with flour. Add another tablespoon of butter to pan. Using tongs, place veal in hot pan. Brown veal on both sides for 1 to 2 minutes. Remove from pan and return onions and mushrooms to pan.
4. Add final tablespoon of butter to pan; place 2 tablespoons of flour used in dusting veal to pan and mix all ingredients together.
5. Add wine and chicken broth while stirring. Return veal to pan, season to taste. Let simmer for 3 to 4 minutes; add parsley.
6. Place veal on plate and pour sauce over each piece. Serve hot.

Yield: 4 servings

Cranberry Glazed Pork

2 pounds pork loin or tenderloin
2 teaspoons cornstarch
¼ teaspoon cinnamon
⅛ teaspoon salt
2 tablespoons orange juice
2 tablespoons dry sherry
1 can whole berry cranberry sauce
½ grated orange peel
1 red onion or Vidalia onion, cut in wedges

1. Preheat oven to 325º.
2. In a small bowl, combine cornstarch, cinnamon, salt and orange juice, stirring until cornstarch is well-blended.
3. Add sherry, orange peel and cranberry sauce. Cook over medium heat until just below boil and sauce starts to thicken. Set aside.
4. Place onion wedges in shallow roasting pan and place pork loin or tenderloin on top of the onions.
5. Put in preheated oven and cook about 45 minutes. Remove from oven and spread half of the cranberry sauce over the onions and roast. Return to oven and continue cooking until meat thermometer registers 155-160º. Let stand few minutes before slicing.
6. Serve with remaining cranberry sauce.

Yield: 6 servings

Apple-Raisins Pork Chops

6 pork chops, boned or boneless
4 medium apples, peeled and sliced
¼ teaspoon thyme
¼ teaspoon nutmeg
3 large onions
1½ tablespoons brown sugar
2 tablespoons raisins
1 bay leaf
1 cup beef stock

1. Preheat oven to 350°.
2. Brown pork chops on both sides in a nonstick pan.
3. Place one-half of onions and apples in casserole. Put pork chops on top; add remaining onion and apple. Sprinkle brown sugar, thyme, nutmeg, raisins and bay leaf on top. Pour beef stock over the apple and pork mixture.
4. Bake for 1 hour.

Yield: 6 servings

America's First Subway

Boston is the birthplace of American mass transportation. In 1897, Boston's Green Line was America's first subway, taking people from Park Street to Boylston Street. The rail line received its name from the beautiful Emerald Necklace park system that the trains passed. Another rail line originally terminated at Harvard University, and since Harvard's colors are crimson and white, that rail line was called the Red Line.

According to the Massachusetts Bay Transportation Authority (MBTA), 14,000 trips carrying over 375,000 passengers over 700 miles are made each and every day.

Pork Chops alla Mafalda
(Castoletti di Maile)

6 pork chops
4 tablespoons flour
1 cup milk
1 cup Italian seasoned bread crumbs
1 (16-ounce) can Italian stewed tomatoes
1 onion, chopped
2 cloves garlic, chopped
4 stalks celery, chopped
1 teaspoon sugar
Salt and pepper

1. Preheat oven to 300°.
2. Trim pork chops of fat, dip each into flour, then milk and finally, the seasoned bread crumbs. Set aside.
3. In a large dutch oven or casserole, combine stewed tomatoes, onion, garlic, celery, sugar and salt and pepper.
4. Place pork chops on top of this mixture. Cover with foil.
5. Bake for 1½ to 2 hours. After chops have been in oven about an hour, check to see if liquid needs to be added. If so, add a little water to pan.
6. Remove the foil. Turn oven on to broil and brown the pork chops on each side for about 5 minutes. Do not over cook.

Yield: 6 servings

"Babson, Babson killed a bear,
With his knife, I do declare"

Home to artists' galleries and quaint shops, Bearskin Neck is a small peninsula in the center of Rockport that juts out into Rockport Harbor, and one of Cape Ann's easternmost points.

Bearskin Neck gets its name from the legend that in 1704, Ebenezer Babson saw a bear attack his nephew. Babson immediately attacked the bear to get its attention away from the young boy. Having no gun, Babson encouraged the bear to follow him into the water. He then killed the bear with a fish knife, brought him onshore, skinned him and spread the hide to dry in the sun, hence the name Bearskin Neck.

Eggplant, Zucchini and Sausage Casserole

½ pound bulk sweet sausage
1 cup eggplant, diced ½-inch
1 cup zucchini, diced ½-inch
½ cup red pepper, diced ½-inch
½ cup yellow pepper, diced ½-inch
¼ cup onion, chopped
2 cloves garlic, minced
4 plum tomatoes, diced
½ cup tomato puree
2 tablespoons fresh parsley
2 tablespoons fresh basil
Pepper to taste
2 ounces grated Mozzarella cheese

1. Preheat oven to 350°.
2. Sauté sausage in a nonstick pan over medium heat, breaking up the meat with a spoon. Remove to a bowl with a slotted spoon; reserve.
3. Add eggplant, zucchini, peppers, onion and garlic to pan. Sauté, stirring occasionally; cook until soft, about 10 to 15 minutes. Stir in the reserved sausage, tomatoes, puree, herbs and seasoning. Reduce the heat and simmer for 15 minutes.
4. Spoon into an oven-to-table casserole dish. Sprinkle with mozzarella cheese.
5. Bake in oven until cheese melts and bubbly, about 30 minutes.

Yield: 6 servings

Swan Boats Glide on Forever

A local Bostonian once wrote, "The Swan Boats are cruising and the ducks are chasing peanuts. It will be just that way for a hundred springs from now, we hope. The New Boston is here and maybe some day there will be a new, new Boston, but good old Boston, like the Swan Boats, quietly glides on forever."

Pork Medallions with Glazed Apples

2½ tablespoons unsalted butter
4 garlic cloves, minced
1 tablespoon dried mustard
1½ tablespoons all-purpose flour
3 cups lowfat, low-salt chicken stock
3 cups lowfat, low-salt beef stock
2 cups apple cider
8 tablespoons butter
8 large apples, cored, cut into 8 wedges
½ cup packed golden brown sugar
2½ pounds pork tenderloin, cut 1-inch thick
2 tablespoons butter
½ cup applejack or apple brandy

1. For the sauce, melt butter in saucepan over medium heat. Add garlic and mustard and sauté for thirty seconds. Add flour and stir two minutes. Gradually whisk in stock and cider. Boil until reduced to sauce consistency, stirring occasionally.
2. To glaze apples, melt 4 tablespoons butter in skillet over medium-high heat. Add half the apples and half the sugar. Sauté until apples soften, about five minutes, place in bowl. Repeat with remaining butter, apples and brown sugar. Combine all apples in skillet.
3. Pound pork between wax paper to ½-inch thickness; coat pork with flour.
4. Melt butter in another skillet over high heat. Add pork in batches; sauté about two minutes per side. Transfer to plate. Return pork to skillet. Remove from heat.
5. Add apple brandy; ignite with match. When flames subside, return skillet to heat and boil until most of the liquid evaporates.
6. Bring sauce to simmer, stirring occasionally and warm apples. Serve pork with apples and cider sauce.

Yield: 8 servings

Roast Leg of Lamb

4 pound leg of lamb,
boned, rolled, tied
1 lemon, cut in half
1 (10-ounce) jar mint jelly
1 tablespoon powdered ginger
1 teaspoon paprika
1 teaspoon salt
1 teaspoon pepper
½ teaspoon garlic powder
1 can beef consommé

1. On the day before roasting, remove excess fat from lamb; cut roast in several places with tip of sharp knife. Rinse well and rub with lemon.
2. Mix jelly with seasonings. Place marinade in large ziplock plastic bag and put roast in bag. Refrigerate overnight, turning occasionally.
3. Preheat oven to 300º. Roast lamb 30 to 35 minutes per pound, basting occasionally.
4. Pour off fat; mix consommé with drippings. Serve au jus.

Cook's Note:
Roast and sauce will be a dark brown.

Yield: 8 to 10 servings

Hamburg Apple Loaf

1 egg, beaten
¼ cup milk
¾ cup bread crumbs
¼ cup chopped onion
2 medium apples-peeled,
cored, and finely chopped
1 teaspoon salt
⅛ teaspoon pepper
⅛ teaspoon ground nutmeg
1½ pounds ground beef

Glaze:
¼ cup ketchup
2 tablespoons brown sugar
1 teaspoon dry mustard
¼ teaspoon ground nutmeg

1. Preheat oven to 350°.
2. Combine all ingredients except ground beef.
3. Add beef, mixing well. Pat into loaf pan.
4. Bake for 75 minutes. Remove from oven.
5. Make glaze by combining ketchup, brown sugar, dry mustard and ground nutmeg. Spread over loaf.
6. Bake an additional 15 minutes.

Keeping Out the Storms

Scientists are trying to determine a way of preserving Venice, Italy from the devastating high tides that periodically flood the historic city. They need look no further than New Bedford for a successful idea. In 1962, the U.S. Army Corps of Engineers built the New Bedford Hurricane Barrier between New Bedford and Fairhaven. The barrier is a 9,100-foot line of rocks, 20-feet above median sea-level, with a 150-foot opening in the center to allow for passing boats and ships. If severe storms or hurricanes threaten the area, two 440-ton gates close the opening to keep out the sea.

Pot Roast with Dried Fruit

3-4 pound round or blade bone roast
1½ teaspoons salt
¼ teaspoon pepper
⅓ cup Burgundy wine
⅓ cup finely chopped carrots
½ cup finely chopped onion
1 clove garlic, minced
1½ cups hot water
1 (11-ounce) package of mixed dried fruit
3 tablespoons all-purpose flour
½ cup cold water

1. Trim fat from meat. Sear all sides of roast in a stockpot.
2. Add salt, pepper, wine, vegetables and garlic. Cook over low heat for 2 hours.
3. Pour hot water over fruit, let stand 1 hour. Drain fruit, reserve liquid. Place fruit on top of meat. Cover and cook 45 to 60 minutes.
4. Remove meat and fruit to platter. Skim fat from pan juice. Add reserved liquid to juices to make 1½ cups.
5. Blend flour and cold water, stir into liquid*. Cook and stir until thickened and boiling. Serve gravy over the meat as desired.

* Add a few tablespoons of hot liquid to flour and water mixture. Stir well before adding to remaining liquid.

Yield: 8 servings

Boeuf Bourguignon

Marinade:
1 large carrot, cut in ½-inch pieces
1 onion, cut in ½-inch pieces
1 celery stalk, cut in ½-inch pieces
2 garlic cloves
Bouquet garni
3 tablespoons brandy
10 black peppercorns
1 bottle of good red wine
2 tablespoons oil

1 (2-pound) chuck steak, trimmed and cut into 1½-inch cubes
1 tablespoon tomato paste, heaped
2 tablespoons flour
1½ cups of brown stock
12 pearl onions
1 tablespoon unsalted butter
½ tablespoon sugar
⅔ cups mushrooms, quartered
2 tablespoons garlic, chopped
½ pound bacon, cut in 2" pieces
2 tablespoons chopped fresh parsley

1. Place all ingredients for the marinade in a bowl with the cubes of beef. Cover and refrigerate overnight.
2. Preheat oven to 400°.
3. Drain marinade into a saucepan, remove the beef and set aside. Make sure that you keep the bouquet garni and vegetables separate. Bring marinade to a boil, skim off the foam, and let boil 6 to 8 minutes. Strain through a fine sieve.
4. In a large, heavy-based casserole dish, heat a little oil and butter. Pat dry beef and brown on all sides in batches, remove and keep to one side. Add the well-drained vegetables from the marinade, lower the heat slightly and cook, stirring occasionally until lightly browned. Return meat to the pan with tomato paste and stir over medium heat for 3 minutes.
5. Sprinkle with flour and place in oven for 6 to 8 minutes. Remove from oven and stir in the flour. Place over medium heat, add marinade and bring to the boil, stirring continuously, then add stock and bouquet garni. Return to the boil, cover and cook in the over for 1 hour and 30 minutes, or until the meat is tender.
6. Place onions, butter, sugar and some salt in a pan and pour in enough water to cover. Cook over medium heat until the water has almost evaporated and swirl the pan until the onions are golden. Fry mushrooms in a little sizzling butter until golden, then season, drain and add to onions. Fry garlic and bacon together in a little oil, drain and add to onions and mushrooms.
7. Once beef is cooked, skim off excess fat. Remove beef to a clean, warm casserole or serving dish, cover and keep warm. Strain sauce and return to the pan, discarding vegetables and bouquet garni. Bring sauce to a boil and simmer for 15 minutes or until the sauce coats the back of a spoon. Season, strain over meat and return to oven for 5 minutes. Add onions, mushrooms and bacon. Sprinkle parsley over the beef and serve hot.

Yield: 4 servings

Cook's Note: A few years ago on a trip to France, I came across this recipe. The preparation takes a bit of time, but the results are definitely worth the work.

The Jared Coffin House

Built by ship owner Jared Coffin as a home for his family in 1845, this house served as an unlikely firebreak during the Great Fire of 1846. Due to its brick construction and slate roof, it resisted the fire that consumed a portion of the center of Nantucket and prevented it from spreading further.

In 1847, the Nantucket Steamship Company bought the house and opened it as a hotel named the Ocean House. It remained the Ocean House until the early 1960s when the Nantucket Historical Trust purchased it. The house was completely renovated and then reopened as the Jared Coffin House. It is a grand place to stay and I have often enjoyed being a guest. During one visit, the island was struck by a nor'easter and I remember feeling quite secure as a group of us spent the evening in the Tap Room.

Baked Stuffed Shrimp

4 ounces butter, not margarine
¼ cup diced celery
¼ cup diced onion
1 cup fresh breadcrumbs
Salt and pepper to taste
Clam juice for moistening
1½ teaspoons of Old Bay® Seasoning
12 jumbo shrimp, deveined and butterflied

1. Slowly sauté celery and onions in butter until onions are transparent. Add salt, pepper and Old Bay® Seasoning. Add breadcrumbs and mix well. Slowly mix in the clam juice until mixture is firm and moist. Do not overmix.
2. Stuff the mixture generously into shrimp and place on a well-greased sheet pan with shrimp tail facing up.
3. Bake at 325-350° until shrimp is cooked and stuffing is browned, approximately 20 to 25 minutes. Baste shrimp and stuffing occasionally with melted butter to keep moist.

Baked Salmon In Cranberry Sauce

2 cups fish stock
⅓ cup cranberry vinegar
¼ cup clarified butter
2 small garlic cloves, minced
2 small shallots, minced
4 (½-pound) salmon fillets
1 cup unsalted butter

1. In a small saucepan, combine fish stock and vinegar; bring to boil. Remove from heat and keep warm.
2. In an ovenproof skillet, heat the clarified butter over medium-high heat and cook garlic and shallots until clear.
3. Add salmon, cook for 1 minute, and turn. Add warm fish stock and cook for 30 seconds longer. Remove from heat; cover skillet with foil.
4. Bake at 425° until salmon flakes with a fork, approximately 30 to 40 minutes. Remove the salmon from the pan. Keep warm while preparing sauce.
5. Place on platter and pour sauce around fillets or serve separately.
6. For cranberry vinegar sauce, return skillet to heat and cook the juices over high heat until reduced to ¾ cup. Reduce heat to low.
7. Whisk in butter, a little at time, to make a smooth sauce.

Baked Haddock

2 pounds fresh haddock
½ cup butter, melted
¼ cup freshly grated Parmesan cheese
1 cup crushed Ritz® crackers
1 tablespoon lemon juice
¼ teaspoon pepper
¼ teaspoon garlic salt
1 tablespoon dry vermouth

1. Preheat oven to 325º.
2. Place haddock in buttered 8-inch baking dish.
3. Mix remaining ingredients together and spoon over haddock.
4. Cover dish and bake for 30 minutes.

Yield: 6 servings

Union Oyster House

Most cities are happy to have one historical restaurant, but Boston is blessed to have many. One of the most famous restaurants is the Union Oyster House. It is the oldest restaurant in continuous service in the United States, serving patrons since 1826. The building was an important contributor to the War of Independence as its owner, Ebenezer Hancock, was the first paymaster of the Continental Army. Today visitors can sit and enjoy their favorite New England specialties in the same rooms as George Washington.

Fried Clams

Vegetable oil
3 eggs
1 cup milk
1 cup flour
Salt
3 cups drained, shucked clams, preferably Ipswich or other long neck, soft shell clam

1. Pour vegetable oil into deep fryer or large heavy pot to a depth of about 3 inches. Heat until temperature reaches 350º. Check with temperature gauge or deep frying thermometer.
2. Preheat oven to the lowest setting. Put paper toweling on cookie sheet to absorb any extra fat.
3. In a dish, beat eggs; add milk to eggs, stirring until well blended. Put seasoned flour in a dish. Put a handful of clams in milk mixture and let them soak for about 1 minute. Take clams and toss them in the flour making sure they are well-coated. Put floured clams in a colander or strainer and shake off any excess flour.
4. With prongs, drop clams into vegetable oil and cook for about two minutes, until golden brown. Make sure to separate clams with a wooden spoon or spatula.
5. Remove from oil and put on paper toweling to absorb extra fat. Remove paper toweling and place clams in oven to keep warm. While the first batch of clams is cooking, soak another handful in milk mixture. This way you will be able to cook the clams faster, so you can enjoy them faster.

Chubby and the Clam

The ubiquitous fried clam was invented on July 3, 1916 at Woodman's in Essex. Whether on purpose or by accident, Lawrence "Chubby" Woodman dropped a clam or two into a fryer while he was making a batch of french fries and lo and behold, the fried clam was born. To true New Englanders, a fried clam *must* have the belly and they must be Ipswich clams; those small, yet ever so succulent, bivalves (shells consisting of two halves, or valves). The Ipswich clam is really a bivalve king, monarch of the mollusks. Dug from tidal flats along the Essex River, the clams must, by law, be taken only by a hand rake and not dredged.

Cataplana Clams

2 pounds small hard-shell clams
4 tablespoons olive oil
3 medium onion, sliced thin
½ teaspoon ground pepper
⅛ - ¼ teaspoon crushed hot pepper
1 large clove garlic, minced
2 bay leaves, broken
¼ cup dry white wine
1 can peeled tomatoes and liquid
8 ounces smoked ham, diced
8 ounces linguica, sliced ½-inch thick
8 tablespoons parsley, chopped
1 pound linguine, cooked al dente

1. Scrub and soak clams 1 hour in cold water. Rinse and drain.
2. Heat olive oil in a cataplana pot with tight cover. Add onions, paprika and peppers. Sauté until onions are limp and golden. Stir in garlic, bay leaf, wine, tomato, ham and linguica; Add clams and half the parsley. Cook over medium heat for 20 minutes.
3. While clams are cooking, prepare linguine according to package directions. Drain and put in a large serving bowl. Top with cataplana mixture. Sprinkle with remaining parsley.

Yield: 8 servings

America's Oldest Seaport

The natural harbor at Gloucester, with its close proximity to the Grand Banks, made it the perfect spot for fisherman and so it became the first seaport of the new colony. For over four centuries, Gloucester has been the story of a great seaport and the schooners that made her famous. Back in the early 1600s, the supply of cod and other cold-water fish seemed inexhaustible, but we now know differently.

Long before the Perfect Storm, men put to sea in boats of all sizes and shapes and many did not return home. At the entrance of the Harbor is the "Man at the Wheel," a statue symbolizing the courage and steadfastness of "they that go down to the sea in ships." Each year thousands of people participate in the blessing of the fleet and to remember those that didn't come home.

Maryland Lump Crab Cakes

1 egg
2 ounces mayonnaise
1 tablespoon parsley, finely chopped
2 teaspoons Worcestershire sauce
1 teaspoon Dijon mustard
1 teaspoon salt
1 teaspoon white pepper
3 ounces fine breadcrumbs
1 pound Maryland lump crab meat
6 ounces flaked crabmeat
2 tablespoons drawn butter

1. Combine egg, mayonnaise, parsley, Worcestershire sauce, mustard, salt and pepper in a bowl; mix well.
2. Mix in breadcrumbs.
3. Fold in crabmeat gently. Shape into six patties.
4. Sauté in drawn butter in skillet until light brown. Serve with spicy mustard sauce.

Yield: 6 servings

Source: Union Oyster House
Boston

Desserts

Boston

Army of Two

In 1810, two young girls, Rebecca and Abigail Bates, saved the town of Scituate. Better known as the "American Army of Two," the girls noticed that two barges filled with Redcoats were headed towards shore. The girls picked up fife and drum and hiding behind a thick cluster of cedar trees, created such a racket that the British mistook them for an entire regiment and decided to make a hasty retreat. This very courageous deed by the young girls saved the town from being sacked by British naval forces during the War of 1812.

Peach and Blueberry Pie

¼ cup sugar
¼ cup brown sugar
3 tablespoons flour
¼ teaspoon cinnamon
⅛ teaspoon salt
2 cups blueberries
2½ cups peaches, sliced
1 tablespoon lemon juice
2 tablespoon butter

1. Preheat oven to 400°.
2. Combine sugar, flour, cinnamon and salt for mixture.
3. Place piecrust in bottom of pie plate and spread blueberries on bottom.
4. Sprinkle half the mixture and half the lemon juice on top. Top with peaches and sprinkle with remaining mixture. Dot with butter.
5. Cover mixture with lattice top crust. Brush lattice with milk. Sprinkle with sugar.
6. Bake for 35 to 40 minutes until brown and bubbly.

Banana Cream Pie

1 (9-inch) pie crust
¾ cup granulated sugar
⅓ cup cornstarch
2½ cups milk
5 egg yolks
1 tablespoon unsalted butter
1 tablespoon vanilla extract
3 large ripe bananas
1½ cups heavy cream

1. Preheat oven to 400º.
2. Line pie shell with foil and fill with dried beans. Bake in oven for 15 minutes; remove foil and beans. Return to oven for another 10 to 15 minutes or until golden brown; cool.
3. Mix ½ cup sugar and cornstarch in heavy-bottomed saucepan. Add milk; cook, stirring over medium heat to thicken, about 5 minutes. Remove from heat.
4. In a small bowl, slowly stir 1 cup of hot mixture into yolks. Stir yolk mixture back into saucepan. Return to medium heat. Bring to boiling, stirring constantly. Cook, stirring for 3 to 5 minutes until very thick; remove from heat.
5. Stir in butter and 2 teaspoons vanilla extract. Place plastic wrap on surface and cool.
6. Slice 1 banana and arrange slices in single layer over bottom of crust. Mash second banana in bowl and stir into custard filling. Pour into crust. Place plastic wrap directly over filling. Refrigerate for 4 hours or until firm.
7. Beat cream, remaining sugar and vanilla extract in bowl until stiff peaks form. Uncover pie. Top with whipped cream. Slice remaining banana and garnish.

Yield: 8 servings

World's Largest Candy Factory

Eight billion sweethearts—those little, heart-shaped candy with the cute sayings— are sold between January 1 and February 14 each year. Annually, more than 4 billion NECCO® Wafers are sold, enough to encircle the globe twice. The New England Confectionery Company (NECCO) in Revere is the largest factory in the world with its entire space devoted to the manufacture of candy. In 1930, Admiral Byrd took 2.5 tons of NECCO® Wafers to the South Pole. That meant that each man at the South Pole could eat nearly a pound of the candy a week for two years.

Strawberry-Rhubarb Pie

3 cups rhubarb, cut in 1-inch pieces
1½ cups strawberries
2½ tablespoons cornstarch
3 tablespoons orange liqueur
1 tablespoon lemon juice
½ teaspoon cinnamon
¾-1 cup sugar
2 tablespoons unsalted butter
Pastry for double-crust 9-inch pie
¼ cup milk

1. Preheat oven to 425°. Line 9-inch pie pan with pastry.
2. Rinse rhubarb and strawberries; drain well.
3. In a bowl, mix cornstarch, orange liqueur, lemon juice and cinnamon until well-blended. Add fruit and sugar; toss to coat. Let stand for 15 to 30 minutes, tossing occasionally.
4. Pour filling into pastry-lined pan; dot with butter.
5. Cut top pastry into ½-inch to ¾-inch strips and form into a lattice top. Brush strips with milk.
6. Bake pie in middle of oven for 15 minutes. Reduce heat to 350° and bake 45 minutes longer, until filling bubbles and crust is golden brown. Serve with frozen yogurt or ice cream.

Yield: 8 servings

Strawberry Cream Pie

1 (9-inch) pie shell
½ cup almond slivers
2½ cups fresh fruit
½ cup water
¼ cup granulated sugar
2 teaspoons cornstarch

Cream Filling:
½ cup granulated sugar
3 tablespoons cornstarch
3 tablespoons flour
½ teaspoon salt
2 cups milk
1 egg, beaten lightly
½ cup heavy cream, whipped
1 teaspoon vanilla extract

1. To make the cream filling, mix granulated sugar, cornstarch, flour and salt. Gradually stir in milk. Stir constantly and bring to boil. Reduce heat and cook and stir until thick.
2. Stir some of hot mixture in with egg, then add back to hot mixture. Bring just to boiling, stirring constantly.
3. Cool, then chill. Beat well and fold in whipped cream and vanilla extract.
4. For the pie, use any fruit that is in season.
5. Toast almonds and sprinkle over pie crust.
6. Fill crust with cream filling. Add 2 cups of fruit on top of cream filling.
7. For the glaze, crush remaining ½ cup of fruit. Add water. Cook 2 minutes. Sieve.
8. Mix sugar and cornstarch.
9. Gradually stir in fruit juice. Cook and stir until thick and clear.
10. Cool slightly and pour over fruit on pie. Keep cool until serving time.

The Book Mill on the Sawmill River

Through the years, the Book Mill building in Montague Center was a gristmill for 100 years, a manufacturing facility for 50 years and a bookstore for the last 15 years. The Sawmill River, which originates at Lake Wyola in Shutesbury, had 22 mills located on it at the height of the Industrial Revolution. Today, several of the mills have been converted to homes, one houses an architectural millwork company and the Kirley sawmill is operational.

The Book Mill is a wonderful place to pass an afternoon. The deck, which overlooks the falls, is a great place to sit with a cup of tea and read. The mill buildings also house the studio gallery of this book's artist, an antique store, a regional craft shop and a marvelous restaurant and cafe.

Coconut Cream Pie

Filling:
4 tablespoons granulated sugar
5 tablespoons flour
¼ teaspoon salt
2 cups milk
3 egg yolks, slightly beaten
1 cup shredded coconut
2 teaspoons vanilla extract
1 (9-inch) baked pie shell
2 egg whites
4 tablespoons granulated sugar
½ cup shredded coconut

1. Combine 4 tablespoons sugar, flour and salt; add milk and egg yolks, mixing thoroughly. Cook until thickened.
2. Add coconut and vanilla extract. Cool slightly, then turn into pie shell.
3. To make the meringue, beat egg whites until foamy throughout.
4. Add 4 tablespoons sugar, 2 tablespoons at a time, beating after each addition until sugar is blended. Continue beating until mixture will stand in peaks.
5. Spread lightly on filling; sprinkle with ½ cup coconut. Bake at 325° for 15 minutes or until lightly browned.

Lemon Meringue Pie

1¼ cups water
1 cup sugar
1 tablespoons butter
⅓ cup cornstarch
3 tablespoons cold water
3 eggs, separated (room temperature)
2 tablespoons milk
6 tablespoons lemon juice
1 teaspoon lemon rind, grated
1 (8-inch) pastry shell
6 tablespoons sugar
1 teaspoon lemon juice

1. Preheat oven to 350º.
2. Combine water, 1 cup sugar, and butter in a heavy saucepan. Cook over medium heat until sugar is dissolved, stirring constantly. Cook and continue stirring, over medium heat until mixture is thickened and transparent, about 5 minutes. Remove from heat.
3. Beat egg yolks with milk; stir a small amount of hot mixture into yolks. Add yolk mixture to hot mixture in saucepan stirring constantly. Cook 2 minutes longer, stirring constantly. Remove from heat and stir in 6 tablespoons lemon and lemon rind. Cool slightly and spoon into pastry shell.
4. Beat egg whites until soft peaks form. Gradually add 6 tablespoons sugar and 1 teaspoon lemon juice, beating until stiff peaks form and sugar is dissolved.
5. Spread meringue over filling, making sure edges are sealed. Bake for 12 to 15 minutes or until golden brown.

French Apple Pie

6 large apples
1 cup sugar
1 tablespoon flour
½ teaspoon nutmeg
½ teaspoon cinnamon
Pinch salt
¾ cup raisins tossed with 1 tablespoon flour
½ cup confectioners sugar

1. Preheat oven to 350°.
2. In pie shell, arrange alternate layers of apples, sugar, spices and raisins. Cover top with thin pastry. Slash top in several places and seal edges.
3. Bake 60 to 70 minutes until pastry is golden.
4. Spread top with confectioners sugar mixed with a tablespoons of water.

For Chocolate Lovers

In 1764, American's love affair with chocolate began when a Harvard graduate, Dr. James Baker, and a young Irishman, John Hannon, formed a partnership. They used a sawmill located on the Neponset River for production. In 1780, they introduced a blend of quality chocolate, Baker's® chocolate, to the marketplace. Fortunately, it is still available today in grocery stores and supermarkets across the country.

Brownies Middleboro

¾ cup flour
¾ teaspoon salt
¼ teaspoon baking powder
1½ - 2 squares Baker's® chocolate
2 eggs
1 cup sugar
¾ teaspoon vanilla
⅓ cup cooking oil
½ cup nuts

1. Preheat oven to 350º.
2. Sift together flour, salt and baking powder; set aside.
3. Melt chocolate either in microwave or on stove in a double boiler.
4. Beat eggs and sugar (one-third at a time); beat after each addition. Add melted chocolate and mix.
5. Add vanilla and cooking oil; beat well.
6. Add flour mixture and stir well. Do not overstir. Add nuts.
7. Place in 9x13-inch baking dish. Bake for 30 minutes. Cook less for chewy brownies; cook longer for cake-like look until tester comes out dry.

Yield: 24 pieces

Fig Newtons®

Besides the beloved chocolate chip Toll House® cookie, the Commonwealth is also known for its famous Fig Newtons® cookie. Over one billion of these delicious cookies are consumed annually. Charles Rosner created the recipe and sold it to Kennedy Biscuit Works in Arlington. The cookies were one of the first commercially baked products to appear on the American market. Named after the town of Newton, which was close to Kennedy Biscuits, it is a soft cookie filled with fig jam and ever so tasty.

Fig-Walnut Rugelach

1 cup unsalted butter, softened
1 (8-ounce) package cream cheese, softened
¼ cup sugar
2 cups all-purpose flour
⅓ cup fig preserves
½ cup chopped walnuts
4 tablespoons granulated sugar

1. Beat butter and sugar in a large bowl with mixer on medium speed until well combined. Reduce speed to low and add sugar and flour; blend well.
2. Divide dough in quarters. Shape each quarter into a 1-inch thick dish. Wrap and refrigerate at least 4 hours or overnight. Make sure dough is firm enough to roll out.
3. When ready to assemble, preheat oven to 350°. Place oven rack in upper third of oven.
4. Melt preserve over low heat, stirring occasionally. Strain to remove large pieces.
5. On a floured surface, roll disk in a 10-inch circle. Brush with preserve, barely covering the dough. Sprinkle with walnuts and sugar.
6. Cut disk into 12 wedges with either a sharp knife or pizza wheel. Roll up each wedge beginning at the widest edge. Place on an ungreased cookie sheet. Repeat with remaining disks.
7. Bake in oven about 20 minutes or until golden brown. Remove to wire rack and cool.

She Loves Me!

In the mid-1800s, Esther Howland made the first Valentine card at her home in Worcester. She imported her supplies from England. Howland wanted her cards to represent a card that she had received in 1847. As the cards became more popular, Howland employed several women to create cards in an assembly-line manner. Eventually, her business grossed $100,000 in sales.

In 1881, Esther Howland retired and sold her company to the George C. Whitney Company which continued to make cards until 1942 when a paper shortage, caused by World War II, caused the company to liquidate.

Valentine Crunchies

½ cup butter
½ cup brown sugar
½ cup sugar
1 egg
½ teaspoon vanilla
1 cup flour
½ teaspoon baking soda
¼ teaspoon salt
¼ teaspoon baking powder
1 cup oatmeal
1 cup cornflakes
½ cup coconut
½ cup chopped pecans

1. Preheat to 350°.
2. Cream butter, add sugar, eggs and vanilla.
3. Sift dry ingredients together and add to creamed mixture.
4. Add cornflakes, oatmeal, coconut and nuts.
5. Roll into small balls and place 2 inches apart on greased cookie sheets.
6. Bake for 10 to 15 minutes.

Banana-Cranberry Oatmeal Cookies

2 ripe medium bananas
¾ cup butter
1½ cups brown sugar, packed
1 egg
½ cup light dairy sour cream
1 teaspoon vanilla
1½ cups all-purpose flour
½ teaspoon baking soda
½ teaspoon salt
½ teaspoon ground cinnamon
¼ teaspoon nutmeg
1½ cups rolled oats
1 cup dried cranberries

1. Preheat oven to 350º.
2. Place bananas in blender. Process until pureed; use 1 cup.
3. Combine dry ingredients: flour, baking soda, salt and spices in a small bowl.
4. Cream butter and add brown sugar in large bowl until light and fluffy.
5. Beat in 1 cup bananas, egg, sour cream and vanilla.
6. Beat in flour mixture until well-blended. Stir in oats and cranberries.
7. Cover and refrigerate dough for 1 hour to firm.
8. Drop batter by heaping tablespoons onto ungreased cookie sheet.
9. Bake 15 to 20 minutes or until cookies are slightly brown around edges.

Yield: 4 dozen cookies

Coconut Kisses

2 large egg whites
Pinch salt
⅛ teaspoon cream of tartar
½ cup confectioners sugar
1 cup sweetened or unsweetened shredded dried coconut
1 teaspoon grated fresh orange or lemon rind

1. Preheat oven to 250º.
2. Beat egg whites in the bowl of an electric mixer. While eggs are still foamy, add salt and cream of tartar. As they begin to stiffen, slowly add sugar. Whip until very stiff.
3. With a rubber spatula, fold in coconut and rind.
4. Line two baking sheets with parchment paper. Place teaspoons of coconut mixture on paper.
5. Bake, rotating baking sheets after 10 minutes, for 20 minutes or until the cookies are delicately browned. Loosen with a spatula and place on racks. Let cookie dry thoroughly.

Yield: 3 dozen

"Ask not what your country can do for you, ask what you can do for your country"

These memorable words came from the inaugural address of John Fitzgerald Kennedy in January 20, 1961. Prior to becoming president, Kennedy served the citizens of Massachusetts as a congressman and U.S. senator. In 1953, he married Jacqueline Bouvier and later became the father of Caroline and John Jr.

President Kennedy called for new civil rights legislation and human rights, and started the Peace Corp to assist developing countries around the world. In 1962, the Cuban Missile Crisis occurred when Russia sought to install nuclear missiles in Cuba. President Kennedy imposed a quarantine on the island and persuaded Moscow to remove the weapons.

In 1963, after only his first one thousand days in office, President Kennedy was assassinated by Lee Harvey Oswald during a motorcade in Dallas. President Kennedy, his wife, children and family have always been held in high esteem in Massachusetts.

Rose Kennedy's Sugar Cookies

½ cup unsweetened butter
¼ cup sugar
3 egg yolks
½ teaspoon vanilla
1 tablespoon milk
1¼ cups all-purpose flour
¼ teaspoon salt
¼ teaspoon baking powder

1. Preheat oven to 375°.
2. Cream butter until light and gradually add sugar.
3. Add egg yolks, vanilla and milk; beat thoroughly.
4. Sift dry ingredients and add to batter in batches. Mix well, but do not overmix.
5. Place on unbuttered cookie sheets by teaspoons. Press down using fingers. If desired, sprinkle top with color sprinkles.
6. Bake in oven for about 8 to 10 minutes, until edges are golden.

Official Cookie of Massachusetts

The most popular cookie of all times has its humble origins in the kitchen at the Toll House Inn in Whitman. Ruth Wakefield was making a batch of Butter Drop Do cookies, a favorite going back to colonial days, when she ran out of nuts and instead chopped up a Nestlé semisweet chocolate bar and added it to the dough. She thought the chocolate would melt, but it didn't and so the Toll House® cookie was born. In a cookbook written by Mrs. Wakefield in 1948, she refers to the cookie as the "Toll House Chocolate Crunch Cookie" and recommends chilling the dough overnight before baking. Since so many love the dough as much as they do the cookies, the bowl could very well be empty in the morning. In 1997, the Massachusetts Legislature named the chocolate chip cookie as the official cookie of the Commonwealth.

Original Toll House® Cookies

1 cup butter
¾ cup brown sugar
¾ cup granulated sugar
2 eggs, beaten
1 teaspoon vanilla
1 teaspoon baking soda
1 teaspoon hot water
2½ cups flour
1 teaspoon salt
1 (12-ounce) bag semisweet chocolate morsels
1 cup nuts (optional)

1. Preheat oven to 375°.
2. Cream butter. Add brown sugar and granulated sugar. Add beaten eggs and vanilla.
3. Dissolve baking soda in teaspoon of hot water.
4. Add flour and salt and sift into mixture alternating with baking soda and water.
5. Stir in morsels and nuts.
6. Drop by teaspoon onto ungreased cookie sheet. Bake for 8 to 12 minutes. The shorter the cooking time, the chewier the cookie.

Yield: 5 to 7 dozen cookies depending on size

Source: Toll House - Tried and True Recipes by Ruth Graves Wakefield

Who or What is a Joe Frogger?

This recipe for molasses-rum cookies goes back over 100 years to the town of Marblehead. They are the inspiration of one man, Uncle Joe, who happened to live on the edge of a frog pond, hence the name Joe Froggers. It seems that Uncle Joe was making a batch of molasses cookies and decided to add a cup of rum to the batter. These large four-inch cookies became an instant hit with young and old alike. Today, we have toned the recipe down a bit by adding rum extract rather than the real thing. Another fun idea is to cut the cookies with a frog-shaped cookie cutter rather than a round one.

Joe Froggers Cookies

4 $\frac{1}{2}$ cups of flour
1 teaspoon baking soda
$\frac{1}{2}$ teaspoon salt
1 teaspoon ginger
$\frac{3}{4}$ teaspoon nutmeg
$\frac{1}{4}$ teaspoon allspice
$\frac{3}{4}$ cup shortening
$\frac{3}{4}$ cup sugar
1 cup light molasses
1 tablespoon rum extract
$\frac{1}{3}$ cup water

1. Preheat oven to 375°.
2. Sift flour, baking soda, salt, ginger, nutmeg and allspice in a medium bowl.
3. Cream sugar and shortening well in a large bowl. Beat in the molasses and rum extract.
4. Add the flour mixture and water alternately, beating until well blended.
5. Wrap dough in plastic wrap and chill overnight. Roll dough $\frac{1}{4}$-inch thick on floured surface. Cut with a 4-inch round cookie cutter.
6. Bake on lightly greased cookie sheet for 8 to 9 minutes.

Banned In Boston

The term "banned in Boston" has been applied to various books and movies throughout the years, but Christmas? Yes, Christmas! The Puritans banned Christmas on May 11, 1659 considering it an invention of the devil. While the law banning Christmas was repealed in 1681, it never became a legal holiday until 1856. This was the same year that Louis Prang, the father of the American Christmas Card, immigrated from Germany to Boston. In 1875, Prang opened a lithographic shop in the Roxbury area and soon after began printing colored cards. By 1881, Prang was printing more that five million cards annually and continued to do so for nearly a decade when he decided he could no longer compete with cheaper imports.

Raspberry Shortbread Cookies

1 cup unsalted butter
⅔ cup granulated sugar
2 large egg yolks
2 teaspoons vanilla extract
2 cups flour, sifted
½ cup raspberry jam

1. Preheat oven to 375º.
2. Cream the butter and sugar until mixture is light in color.
3. Add the egg yolks and beat until mixture is fluffy. Stir in vanilla.
4. Gradually add the flour.
5. Roll one teaspoon of dough into a ball, place on an ungreased cookie sheet and pat flat with fingertips. Using your thumb, make a well in the center of each cookie.
6. Spoon raspberry jam into each indentation.
7. Bake about 8 to 10 minutes or until cookie edges turn a light golden brown.

Yield: 4 dozen

Massachusetts' Finest

Massachusetts fans are among the most loyal sports fans in the country. Where else would you pay the highest ticket prices in baseball to see a team that hasn't won a World Series since the days of Babe Ruth (1918)? Yet it is almost impossible to get tickets to see a Red Sox game.

The Red Sox were supposedly cursed by Babe Ruth when he was transferred to New York; in these here parts it is know as the "Curse of the Bambino." The Red Sox were sold in 2002 and it is hoped that the curse has finally been lifted, but only time will tell. As I write, the curse is still on.

In 2002 and again in 2004, the New England Patriots won the Super Bowl. Most of us still can't get over the fact that one of our four professional teams actually won a championship, let alone two in two years. It has been years since the Celtics won a championship and even longer for the Bruins.

Strawberries with Crème Fraiche

In late spring, native strawberries start appearing at farmers markets and roadside stands. Ever so sweet and juicy, they are enjoyed by all.

Fresh strawberries, hulled
Crème fraiche
Brown sugar

Crème Fraiche:
1 cup heavy cream
½ cup sour cream

1. Place several whole berries upright in a bowl, spoon crème fraiche over berries and sprinkle with brown sugar.
2. Whisk creams together in a small container. Cover with airtight lid and let stand in a warm spot for about 12 hours. Stir the crème fraiche and refrigerate for at least 24 hours before serving.

The Bridge of Flowers

The Bridge of Flowers was built in 1908 as a trolley bridge for the Shelburne Falls & Colrain Street Railway to cross the Deerfield River. For 20 years trolleys used the bridge to haul freight between the rail yard in Shelburne and several textile mills in Colrain. After the railway went out of business in 1928, a group of dedicated gardeners raised funds to turn it into a 400-foot bridge of flowers. Visited by about 25,000 people annually, it is the only known bridge in the world that solely grows flowers. The Shelburne Falls Women's Club maintains over 500 varieties of flowers, vines and shrubs on the bridge — from tulips and daffodils in April to chrysanthemums in October.

Grape-Nut Custard Pudding

9 eggs
1 gallon light cream
2 cups sugar
2 tablespoons vanilla extract
1 cup Grape-Nuts® cereal
1 teaspoon nutmeg
1 teaspoon cinnamon

1. Preheat the oven to 325º.
2. Whip eggs, cream, sugar and vanilla completely with a wire whisk or mixer.
3. Pour the mixture into a 9x12-inch pan.
4. Sprinkle Grape-Nuts®, nutmeg and cinnamon evenly over top.
5. Place the 9x12-inch pan into a large pan to form a water bath (fill with water to the height of the custard mixture).
6. Gently place in heated oven for approximately 90 minutes.
7. Let cool and serve warm or chilled with whipped cream and a sprinkle of cinnamon.

Cook's Note:
Oven temperature will greatly affect cooking time. Check for doneness by gently wiggling the pan. Remove from oven as soon as center of the custard begins to gel.

Red Sox and Fenway Park

Home of the beloved Red Sox baseball team, Fenway Park is the last of the stadiums built in the Golden Age of ballparks (1909–1915). Fenway's opening day was on April 20, 1912. Fenway is so named because of where it is built, in an area of Bosont knows as the Fens. Four world championships were won in this park, though most people alive today haven't seen one. There have been several attempts by the owners to replace Fenway with a modern updated glitzy park, but most Bostonians love their history and want Fenway to remain right where it is.

Several Hall of Famers have called Fenway home, including Ted Williams, Carl Yastrzemski, Carlton Fisk, Cy Young and Babe Ruth. Fenway only seats about 34,000 people, but it is a cozy place on a warm summer evening to sit and enjoy a game.

Rice Pudding

½ cup long-grain, uncooked
6 cups milk
¼ teaspoon salt
3 eggs, beaten
⅓ cup sugar
1 teaspoon vanilla extract
1 cup raisins
Nutmeg

1. Preheat over to 350º.
2. Rinse rice well and set aside.
3. Scald 4 cups milk, making sure to skim foam from top.
4. Add rice. Add salt and cook over medium heat until mixture thickens, stirring constantly.
5. Add eggs, sugar, vanilla and remaining milk. Stir in raisins and mix well.
6. Transfer mixture to a greased 2-quart casserole dish. Sprinkle with nutmeg.
7. Bake for 1 hour.

Yield: 8 to 10 servings

Baked Apples in Brandy Sauce

8 apples, cored
1 cup brown sugar, packed
½ teaspoon ground cinnamon
¼ teaspoon ground nutmeg
⅛ teaspoon ground allspice
1 cup brandy

1. Preheat oven to 350°.
2. Place cored apples in 13x9x2-inch baking dish.
3. In saucepan, combine sugar and spices, stir in brandy. Bring to a slow boil over medium-high heat.
4. Pour three-quarters of brandy sauce over apples. Cover and bake for 25 to 30 minutes or until apples are fork-tender.
5. Place apples in dessert bowls.
6. Warm extra brandy sauce and pour over apples just before serving.

Yield: 8 servings

Brigham's Hot Fudge Sauce

¼ cup butter
1½ squares unsweetened chocolate
¾ cup granulated sugar
¼ cup unsweetened cocoa powder
Dash salt
½ cup all-purpose cream or evaporated milk
1 teaspoon vanilla

1. Over low heat, melt butter and chocolate.
2. Mix sugar, cocoa and salt. Add to chocolate mixture.
3. Mix together until smooth. Slowly add cream and bring to a boil, stirring constantly.
4. Remove from heat immediately and add vanilla.

Yield: 3 cups

When is a Pie, Not a Pie?

The Parker House in Boston is known mostly for its Parker House rolls, but their delicious Boston Cream Pie (which is really a cake) was first noticed on its menu in 1856. Food historians feel that the pie got its name from colonists who actually baked cakes in pie tins, as most did not have cake pans. The first reference to the dessert was in an article in a New York newspaper that referred to a pudding pie cake. The recipe for this dessert had a powdered sugar topping and it wasn't until it appeared on the menu at the Parker House that the tasty chocolate glaze was used. So is it a pie or is it a cake? You decide; either way it is delicious.

Boston Cream Pie

Cake:
1½ sticks unsalted butter, room temperature
1¼ cups sugar
1 teaspoon vanilla
2 large eggs
2 cups cake flour
2½ teaspoons baking powder
½ teaspoon salt
¾ cup milk

Custard:
3 tablespoons corn starch
⅓ cup sugar
1 cup milk
3 large eggs
½ cup heavy cream
¼ teaspoon salt
1 vanilla bean, split lengthwise
3 tablespoons unsalted butter

Glaze:
6 ounces bittersweet chocolate
3 tablespoons water
2 tablespoons unsalted butter
1½ tablespoons corn syrup
¼ teaspoon salt

1. Preheat oven to 350°. Prepare a 9½-inch springform pan.
2. In a medium bowl, cream together butter, sugar and vanilla until light and fluffy. Beat in 2 eggs, one at a time, beating well after each.
3. In a separate bowl, sift together flour, baking powder and salt and beat into butter mixture in batches alternating with milk, and beginning and ending with flour mixture.
4. Pour batter into prepared pan and bake in the middle of oven for 50 to 60 minutes or until an inserted tester comes out clean. Let cake cool in pan on a rack.
5. To make the custard, in a saucepan whisk together cornstarch, sugar and milk. Add eggs, cream and salt, and whisk the mixture until smooth. Add seeds from vanilla bean, reserving the pod, to cream mixture and bring to a boil over moderate heat, whisking constantly, for 2 minutes.
6. Remove pan from heat and whisk butter. Let custard cool completely, whisking occasionally.
7. To make the glaze, in a double-boiler melt chocolate with water, butter, corn syrup and salt, stirring until the glaze is smooth. Remove from heat when melted through.
8. To assemble, remove cake from the pan and cut in half horizontally. Place bottom half on a plate. Top bottom half with custard, spreading it to the edge.
9. Put the remaining cake half, cut side down, on custard and pour glaze on top, spreading it to the edge and letting it drip down the sides.

Source: Parker House
Boston

Thar She Blows!

Humans aren't the only mammals that enjoy the warm waters of the Gulf Stream as it passes Cape Cod. The Stellwagen Bank National Marine Sanctuary is the summer home of many humpback, finbacks and minke whales. It isn't for the beauty of the area that they come, but for the feeding grounds of the sanctuary.

I still remember my first whale-watching trip on a cold fall day. These gentle giants were gathering and having their final feast before heading south for the winter. Everyone on the boat from the Dolphin Fleet in Provincetown had seen a whale but me. I was lamenting this point to naturalist John Green when he quietly suggested that I turn around slowly. There, not ten feet from me, was a humpback whale checking us out (this is called spyhopping). The whale then winked at me as he slid quietly below the surface. It was a special moment that I will always treasure.

Cranberry Crisp

2 cups cranberries
½ cup chopped walnuts
½ cup sugar
¾ cup melted butter
1 cup sugar
2 eggs, beaten
1 teaspoon almond extract
1 cup flour

1. Preheat oven to 325°.
2. Place cranberries, chopped walnuts and sugar in bottom of a 10-inch greased pie plate.
3. Mix melted butter, sugar, eggs, almond extract and flour together and spread over cranberry mixture.
4. Bake for 35 to 40 minutes.

Yield: 6 servings

Little Grey Lady of the Sea

During the early 1800s, the island of Nantucket was considered the whaling capital of the world. At its pinnacle, over eighty whaling ships called Nantucket home. Herman Melville got his idea for *Moby Dick* from the tragedy of the Essex, which was broadsided by a whale off the coast of South Africa. Three events coincided to bring the good times to an end for the island: the Great Fire of 1846, dwindling demand for whale oil and the discovery of gold in California.

Today Nantucket is one of the best-known tourist destinations in New England. People go for a variety of reasons to visit the "Little Grey Lady of the Sea." There are the daffodils in the spring, millions of daffodils which bloom from mid-April into May; lovely roses that grow over many of the homes in Siasconcet during the summer; and finally the Christmas walk during the first week of December. Many enjoy visiting the island after the tourists leave when the population drops from over 50,000 to around 9,000 people.

Strawberry-Chocolate Sauce

1 pound strawberries, hulled
3 tablespoons butter
¼ cup walnuts, finely chopped
3 tablespoons dark brown sugar
3 tablespoons grated semisweet chocolate

1. Melt butter in medium skillet.
2. Add walnuts and cook for one minute.
3. Add dark brown sugar and stir for 30 seconds. Remove from heat.
4. Stir in the berries and grated semisweet chocolate.
5. Spoon over ice cream for a delicious treat.

Out of Beer

"We could not now take much time for further search, our victuals being much spent, especially our beer," according to an entry in the diary of William Bradford, the first governor of Massachusetts Bay Colony. It seems that the Pilgrims stopped and went ashore not for the beauty of the area, but because they were running low on beer. The first Thanksgiving would have been held further south, most likely in Virginia, if not for this little known fact.

Cherries Jubilee

½ cup sugar
2 tablespoons corn starch
⅛ teaspoon salt
1½ cups bing cherries, pitted
1 cup cherry juice
2 teaspoons lemon juice
¼ teaspoon lemon rind
¼ teaspoon almond extract
⅓ cup brandy or kirsch

1. Mix a little water together with cornstarch to make a thick paste and combine with salt, sugar and cherry juice in a saucepan over medium heat. Stir well until mixture becomes clear and nicely thickened.
2. Gradually stir in the lemon juice, lemon rind, almond extract, brandy and bing cherries.
3. At this point, you can transfer the cherries jubilee to a heated chafing dish for serving. For a dramatic presentation, as you are ready to serve, pour a little additional brandy and ignite with long matchstick. Make sure you do this where it is safe, not close to anything flammable or near any people.
4. Delicious over ice cream, or on top of pound or angel food cake.

Yield: 6 servings

Peach Cobbler

½ cup unsalted butter or margarine
1 egg
1 cup milk
1 teaspoon vanilla extract
1 cup sugar
1 cup all-purpose flour
1 teaspoon baking powder
2 teaspoons salt, or to taste
4 cups fresh peaches, sliced

1. Preheat oven to 375°.
2. Melt butter slowly in a 9x13-inch baking pan over low heat. Tilt to spread evenly.
3. In a bowl, mix egg, milk and vanilla. Add sugar, flour, baking powder and salt and mix thoroughly.
4. Pour batter evenly over melted butter (do not blend or mix). Arrange fruit evenly over the batter.
5. Bake for 45 minutes or until crust is golden brown. Remove from oven and serve warm with either cream or ice cream.

Yield: 6 servings

Peach Melba

1 (10-ounce) package frozen raspberries
¼ cup sugar
⅓ cup water
1 tablespoon cornstarch
1 tablespoon water
6 peach halves

1. Crush raspberries; add sugar and water with a pinch of salt. Bring to boiling point and strain.
2. Mix cornstarch and water until smooth. Add to hot juices slowly and cook until sauce thickens and clears.
3. Place half a peach in bottom of the dessert dish. Arrange a scoop of vanilla or peach ice cream in center. Cover with melba sauce.

Yield: 6 servings

Mary Had a Little Lamb

The father of young Mary Elizabeth Sawyer gave her a young lamb that had been rejected by its mother and Mary wanted to try and save its life. As the lamb grew stronger, it started to follow Mary everywhere. One day the lamb followed Mary to school in the Central Massachusetts town of Sterling. A neighbor upon hearing the tale wrote the verse we all learned in school:

Mary had a little lamb,
Its fleece was white as snow...

Tipsy Parson

6 egg yolks
4 cups scalded milk
½ cup sugar
Dash of salt
1 teaspoon vanilla
1 (10-inch) round angel food cake
1 cup almonds, slivered
1 cup sherry
1 pint whipping cream
1 tablespoon sugar
Maraschino cherries

1. Lightly beat egg yolks in the top of a double boiler. Add scalded milk, sugar and salt; cook over (not in) hot water. Do not let water boil. Stir constantly until the sauce coats the spoon.
2. Add vanilla extract, remove from heat and let mixture cool.
3. Cut angel cake horizontally into three slices. Place one slice in the bottom of a glass trifle dish or large bowl. Stick half of almonds in it; pour ¼ cup sherry over it. Spoon some custard over it and place the second layer of cake on top; repeat process. After adding the top layer, pour on more sherry and add remaining custard.
4. Whip cream until stiff, adding sugar and a bit of sherry. Cover custard with whipped cream. Add cherries for decoration and refrigerate until ready to serve.

Yield: 10 to 12 servings

Chocolate Stout Cake

2 cups stout (such as Guinness)
2 cups unsalted butter
1½ cups unsweetened cocoa powder (preferably Dutch)
4 cups all purpose flour
4 cups sugar
1 tablespoon baking soda
1½ teaspoons salt
4 large eggs
1⅓ cups sour cream

Icing:
2 cups whipping cream
1 pound bittersweet or semisweet chocolate, chopped

1. Preheat oven to 350º.
2. Butter three (8-inch) round cake pans with 2-inch high sides. Line with parchment paper. Butter paper.
3. Bring 2 cups stout and 2 cups butter to simmer in heavy large saucepan over medium heat.
4. Add cocoa powder and whisk until mixture is smooth. Cool slightly.
5. Whisk flour, sugar, baking soda and 1½ teaspoons salt in large bowl.
6. Using an electric mixer, beat eggs and sour cream in another large bowl to blend. Add stout-chocolate mixture to egg mixture and beat just to combine.
7. Add flour mixture and beat briefly on slow speed.
8. Using rubber spatula, fold in stout/butter until completely combined. Divide batter equally among prepared pans.
9. Bake cakes until tester inserted into center of cakes comes out clean, about 35 minutes. Transfer cakes to rack; cool 10 minutes. Turn cakes out onto rack and cool completely.
10. Place one cake layer on plate and spread ⅔ cup icing over top of cake. Place second cake layer on top of first and spread ⅔ cup icing on top of this layer. Top with third cake layer and spread remaining icing over top and sides of cake.
11. For icing, bring cream to simmer in heavy medium saucepan. Remove from heat.
12. Add chopped chocolate and whisk until melted and smooth. Refrigerate until icing is spreadable, stirring frequently, about 2 hours.

Source: Barrington Brewery & Restaurant
Great Barrington

Quabbin Reservoir

In the late 1930s when Greater Boston found itself running short of drinking water, it was decided to flood the Swift River Valley. About 2,500 people were forced to abandon their homes and land when their property was taken by eminent domain. Tens of thousands of acres were taken, 13 cemeteries were relocated and buildings were razed. Today the towns of Dana, Enfield, Prescott and Greenwich lay beneath the pristine waters of the reservoir.

The North Prescott church (below), one of a few buildings saved from the flooding, was moved from the Quabbin and is now in nearby New Salem. It is home to the Swift River Valley Historical Society.

Today the 39-square mile reservoir, which holds 412 billion gallons of water, is a 58,000-acre wildlife reservation. It is the largest man-made reservoir in the world used exclusively for water supply.

Dutch Apple Cake

1 cup flour
2 teaspoons baking powder
½ teaspoon salt
⅓ cup butter, softened
1 egg
1 cup milk
5 apples, cored and pared
¼ cup sugar

1. Preheat oven to 350°.
2. Mix and sift flour, baking powder and salt. Rub in the butter with a fork or pastry cutter.
3. Beat egg and add to milk; stir into the dry ingredients, making a dough soft enough to spread ½-inch thick in a shallow baking tin (9x13-inch pan).
4. Cut apples into eighths; lay them on top of the dough in parallel rows with sharp edges down. Sprinkle top with sugar and a touch of cinnamon.
5. Bake for 30 minutes or until cake tester inserted into the middle comes out clean.
6. Serve warm with lemon, blueberry, strawberry or raspberry sauce.

Source: The Quabbin Cookbook (1916)
Submitted by A.E.B.

Ribbon Cake

If you notice, no oven temperature is noted. It always referred to as either a "hot oven" or a "not too hot oven" or "moderate oven" or "very hot." Most of these ladies cooked using a wood stove and oven, so it wasn't possible to regulate the oven temperature. I wonder how today's cooks would succeed if they had to cook in this manner. This recipe was reproduced as it was submitted for the cookbook almost ninety years ago.

Cream ½ cup butter, add 1½ cups sugar, yolks of 2 eggs, 2½ cups flour sifted with 2 level tablespoons cream tartar and ½ teaspoon soda, ½ cup milk and white of 3 eggs beaten stiff. Bake one-third of the mixture as a white layer cake. To the balance, add 2 tablespoons maple syrup, ½ cup each chopped raisins and nuts, add cinnamon and clove to taste. Bake this part in two layers. Put together with currant jelly. Frost with boiled maple dressing.

Source: The Quabbin Cookbook (1916)
Submitted by Sada E. Smith

The Silent Island

Today when we think of Martha's Vineyard, we think what a wonderful place to live or visit. But for over 300 years, a large portion of the year round residents of the island could not hear. For example, in 1854 the national average was one deaf person in 5,728; on the Vineyard it was one in 155; and in the tiny town of Chilmark it was one in 25.

The deafness was probably due to an inbred recessive gene and since most islanders at that time, were born, lived and died on the Vineyard, the gene was simply transfered from one family to another, from one generation to the next. Imagine living in such a beautiful place and not being able to hear the seagulls, nor the winds through the trees or the waves crashing upon the shore. Unfortunately, for thousands of islanders, it was a reality.

Pineapple Cheese Cake

1 package Zwieback
¼ cup sugar
2 ounces butter, melted
1 can crushed pineapple
1½ pounds cream cheese
1 cup sugar
1 teaspoon vanilla
3 eggs
½ pint sour cream
2 tablespoons sugar
1 teaspoon vanilla
Cinnamon

1. Preheat oven to 350º.
2. Crumble Zwieback, sugar and butter together, spread in 9x13-inch glass baking dish. Bake for 8 to 10 minutes. Drain pineapple and spread over the crust.
3. Beat together cream cheese, 1 cup sugar, 1 teaspoon vanilla and eggs. Pour over pineapple and bake for 30 minutes.
4. Mix sour cream, 2 tablespoons sugar and 1 teaspoon vanilla with spoon and pour over baked cream cheese. Sprinkle cinnamon and sugar over it and bake for 10 minutes.

Yield: 15 to 18 servings

Seabiscuit

Once upon a time there was a famous racehorse named Seabiscuit. This fabulous horse by all appearances would never be named 1938 Horse of the Year, yet he was. The 1930s were a time when there was not a great deal to cheer about, but this marvelous horse could draw people by the thousands to watch him race. In one year, Seabiscuit had more news coverage than several famous figures including Roosevelt, Hitler and Mussolini.

In 1937, Seabiscuit won the Massachusetts Handicap at Suffolk Downs in East Boston. In 2003, a bronze plaque honoring this special horse was placed at the entrance to the clubhouse.

Gingerbread

2 teaspoons baking powder
1½ cups flour, sifted
1 teaspoon ginger
¼ teaspoon cinnamon
¼ teaspoon nutmeg
⅛ teaspoon ground clove
⅛ teaspoon mace
¼ teaspoon salt
⅓ cup sugar
½ stick butter
½ cup boiling water
½ cup molasses
½ cup raisins (optional)

1. Preheat oven to 325°. Grease and flour an 8-inch square pan.
2. Sift baking powder, flour, and spices together into a large mixing bowl.
3. Melt butter in saucepan, add sugar, water and molasses. Heat slowly until mixture comes to a boil; then boil for 2 to 3 minutes.
4. Cool and gradually add to the dry ingredients, stirring constantly.
5. Spread in greased pan and bake 35 minutes.

Yield: 8 servings

Dory - The Diamond Shaped Boat

In 1783, a strange flat-bottom marquis-shaped boat, better known as a dory, began its humble origins at Lowell's Boat Shop in Amesbury. Anyone who ever saw Spencer Tracy in the Old Man and the Sea knows what a dory looks like. The Lowell Boat Shop still operates and is the oldest boat builder in the nation. Since its inception, tens of thousands of dories and skiffs have been crafted through several generations of the Lowell family. Today the Newburyport Maritime Society operates the Boat Shop as a nonprofit company.

Pumpkin Cake Roll

3 eggs
1 cup granulated sugar
⅔ cup pumpkin
1 teaspoon lemon juice
¾ cup flour
1 teaspoon baking powder
2 teaspoons cinnamon
1 teaspoon ginger
½ teaspoon nutmeg
½ teaspoon salt

Filling:
1 cup confectioners sugar
2 (3-ounce) packages cream cheese
4 tablespoons butter
½ teaspoon vanilla

1. Preheat oven to 375°. Grease and flour a 15x10x1-inch pan.
2. Beat egg on high speed of mixer for five minutes; gradually beat in sugar. Stir in pumpkin and lemon juice.
3. Stir together flour, baking powder, cinnamon, ginger, nutmeg and salt. Fold into pumpkin mixture. Spread in pan and bake for 15 minutes.
4. Turn out on a towel sprinkled with powdered sugar. Starting at narrow end, roll towel and cake together; cool. Unroll gently.
5. Combine sugar, cream cheese, butter and vanilla. Beat until smooth. Spread over cake and roll. Sprinkle top with confectioners sugar. Chill.

Lemon Pound Cake

1½ cups unsalted butter, room temperature
1 (8-ounce) package cream cheese, softened
3 cups sugar
¼ cup fresh lemon juice
1½ tablespoons vanilla extract
1 tablespoon lemon peel, grated
6 large eggs
3 cups all purpose flour
¼ teaspoon salt
1¾ cups powdered sugar
3 tablespoons milk
1 tablespoon fresh lemon juice

1. Preheat oven to 350º. Grease and flour 10-inch diameter angel food pan.
2. Cream butter in large bowl with electric mixer until light; add cream cheese and beat until well combined.
3. Add sugar and beat until light and fluffy, about 3 minutes. Add lemon juice, vanilla and lemon peel.
4. Add 2 eggs at a time; beat until combined. Add flour and salt and beat just until batter is smooth and creamy.
5. Spoon batter into prepared pan. Bake for 1½ hours or until tester inserted near center comes out clean. Cool cake in pan on rack 15 minutes. Turn out cake onto rack and cool.
6. For glaze, mix powdered sugar, milk, and fresh lemon juice in a small bowl until smooth. Spoon sauce over cake, allowing glaze to drip down sides. Let stand until glaze sets, about 30 minutes.

Yield: 12 to 15 servings depending on size

Toasted Angel Food With Orange Sauce

½ cup butter, softened
1½ cups sugar
4 egg yolks
⅔ cup milk
1 tablespoon grated orange rind
⅔ cup orange juice
1 (10-inch) round angel food cake

1. Mix butter and sugar in top of double boiler. Beat in yolks one at a time. Stir in orange rind, orange juice and milk.
2. Cook over hot water 10 to 15 minutes. Cool; sauce will be thin.
3. Cut angel food cake into number of slices as needed. Brush both sides with melted butter. Set slices on baking sheet and toast both sides under broiler.

Pastel de Tres Leches
(Cake with Three Milks)

¼ cup butter, melted and cooled
6 large eggs, separated
¼ teaspoon baking soda
¼ teaspoon salt
1 cup sugar
1 cup all-purpose flour
2½ cups milk
1 (12-ounce) can evaporated milk
1 (14-ounce) can sweetened, condensed milk
2 cups whipping cream

1. Preheat oven to 350°. Generously butter a 9x13-inch baking pan.
2. Combine egg whites, baking soda and salt; beat until soft peaks form (about 2 to 3 minutes).
3. Add yolks to the whites and beat until completely combined. With mixer on low speed, gradually add sugar until well blended.
4. Using a rubber spatula, fold in butter.
5. Sift ¼ cup flour on top of mixture and gently fold in to combine. Repeat with remaining flour, folding in ¼ cup at a time.
6. Pour batter into greased pan and bake about 20 to 25 minutes, or until a cake tester inserted into the middle comes out clean.
7. Whisk together three milks and pour over cake upon removing from oven. Run spatula around edges to loosen cake, but set cake aside and let it cool. Cover cake and refrigerate at least five hours, or overnight.
8. When ready to serve, whip cream to soft peaks. Serve with cake along with delicious raspberries, fresh pineapple, mango, blueberries or other fruits.

Preserves and More

(c) LTM

The Ubiquitous Grape

In 1849, Ephraim Wales Bull developed the perfect and palatable grape and named it the Concord, after the town where it was grown. The Concord was the result of a 22,000-seedling crossbreeding experiment of 125 vines. In 1869, a dentist, Dr. Thomas Welch, along with his family, produced an unfermented sacramental wine for their church in New Jersey. This led to the beginning of the processed fruit juice industry and Welch's® Grape Jelly.

Grape Jelly

8 pounds Concord grapes
8 pounds sugar

1. Wash jars and lids in hot soapy water; rinse and sterilize by boiling in water for 15 minutes (leave in water until needed). Lids may be sterilized by placing them in boiling water; boil 5 minutes (leave in warm water until needed). Utensils should also be sterilized.
2. Pick over grapes; wash and drain. Mash in the bottom of a preserving kettle until well mashed. Heat burner slowly and cook slowly until juice is removed, drawn out (about 30 minutes).
3. Strain through a coarse strainer; then allow juice to drop through a double thickness of cheesecloth or a jelly bag.
4. Measure juice, return to pan and bring to boiling point. Boil five minutes; add an equal measure of sugar. Boil until surface looks wrinkled and the liquid jellies on the edge.
5. Skim well, and pour into glasses. Cover and seal. Store and keep in a cool, dry place.

Yield: 4 pints

Famous Little Red Berry of Massachusetts

Is it "crane berry" or cranberry? Some historians claim the cranberry got its name because cranes were often seen eating the berries. Others suggest its name originated from its slender stem and pink blossoms that resembled the neck and head of a crane. The word cranberry first appeared in 1647 in a letter written by missionary John Eliot. Cranberry sauce as a food was first mentioned in 1680 in a letter written to a relative in England from a settler in New Jersey. The settler wrote a recipe for taking cranberries and making it into a sauce. Often times the settlers added maple syrup to sweeten the tart cranberry.

Cranberry Orange Sauce

1 cup sugar
¾ cup water
3 cups cranberries
¼ cup dry white wine
1½ teaspoons orange peel, finely shredded
3 tablespoons orange juice
¼ teaspoon ground cinnamon
1 cinnamon stick

1. Mix sugar and water together in a saucepan. Bring to a boil.
2. Add cranberries, white wine, orange peel, orange juice and cinnamon stick. Bring to boil; reduce heat. Simmer uncovered for 15 minutes.
3. Remove from heat. Cook mixture slightly. Place mixture in blender or processor; blend about thirty seconds or until smooth.
4. Return to saucepan and add cinnamon stick. Simmer, uncovered, until slightly thickened.

Yield: 2½ cups

Hoops Anyone?

While at Springfield College, Dr. James Naismith was given the dubious task of developing a new indoor game for students to play during the winter months. At that time, it is doubtful if he had any idea what the future would hold.

Dr. Naismith had just two weeks to perform the task, and on the final day he came up with a new game that had 13 rules and was played with a soccer ball, peach basket and nine players on each team. Little did the students who played this first game know, but they were now part of sports history and 101 years later, a new shrine to the stars of the sport would open just a few miles from where the game began.

In 1968, the first Basketball Hall of Fame opened on the campus of Springfield College. Over the next fifteen years, the Hall outgrew itself and so a new Hall was built in downtown Springfield. An even larger Hall opened in 2002 with much fanfare and many basketball greats present, including Larry Bird and Magic Johnson.

Lemon Sauce

½ cup sugar
4 teaspoons cornstarch
⅛ teaspoon nutmeg
1 cup water
2 tablespoons butter
½ teaspoon lemon peel, finely shredded
2 tablespoons lemon juice

1. In a small saucepan, stir together sugar, cornstarch and nutmeg. Stir in water and cook, stirring constantly, until sauce thickens and is bubbly. Continue to cook for two more minutes.
2. Add butter, lemon peel and lemon juice. Stir until butter melts. Serve warm over gingerbread, pancakes, etc.

Yield: 1¼ cups

Peach Butter

½ cup peaches, fresh or frozen
1 tablespoon orange juice
1 tablespoon sugar
½ pound salted butter

1. Dice peaches and in a small saucepan bring the peaches, orange juice and sugar to a boil. Lower heat and continue cooking until peaches are tender and mixture is cooked down to a jam-like consistency. Let cool.
2. Let butter softened to room temperature. Mix peaches and butter together until well blended.
3. Place butter in either a crock or glass-serving dish. Cover and chill until ready to serve. Let soften before using.

Cook's Note: Peach butter is delicious on popovers, waffles and french toast.

Cranberry Cointreau Chutney

2 cups fresh cranberries
¾ cup brown sugar, packed
½ cup water
½ cup light raisins
½ cup celery, chopped
2 tablespoons finely chopped candied ginger
¼ cup walnuts, chopped
½ cup apple, chopped
2 tablespoons lemon juice
1 teaspoon onion salt
¼ teaspoon ground cloves
¼ cup Cointreau or Grand Marne

1. In a large saucepan, combine all ingredients. Bring to boil, stirring constantly. Reduce heat. Simmer uncovered for 15 minutes, stirring occasionally.
2. Cover and store in the refrigerator. Serve chilled.

Yield: 3 cups

Off By Less Than an Inch

In 1851, two separate work crews began digging a 4.8-mile tunnel through Hoosac Mountain between the Western Massachusetts towns of North Adams and Florida. During the 22 years of construction, nearly 200 men died and over 1.9 million tons of rock was blasted and removed from the mountain. When the two crews met on November 28, 1873, their alignment was off by merely nine-sixteenth of an inch — a record for tunnel accuracy still held today. Unlike the Big Dig of Boston, the Hoosac Tunnel cost $17 million and came in on budget.

Peach Chutney

4 cups peaches, peeled, pitted and chopped
¾ cup vinegar
3 cups lemon juice
1 cup raisins
1 cup raisins, chopped
2 cups garlic cloves, minced
3 cups ginger
1 tablespoon salt
1 teaspoon allspice
2 teaspoon cinnamon
2 teaspoon cloves, ground
2 teaspoon ginger, ground
7½ cups sugar
1 bottle liquid pectin

1. To peel peaches, immerse a few at a time in a pot of boiling water for a few minutes. Remove peaches and dip them in a bowl of ice water. The peel will come off quite easy with a paring knife.
2. Place peaches in a large non-reactive stock pot.
3. Add vinegar, lemon juice, raisins, onions, garlic, salt, spices, and sugar. Mix thoroughly. Put over high heat and bring to a rolling boil, stirring occasionally. Boil hard for one minute, stirring constantly. Remove from heat.
4. Stir pectin in immediately. Skim off the foam with a metal spoon. Stir and skim for five minutes to cool slightly and prevent floating fruit.
5. Ladle into hot sterilized jelly glasses. Pour ⅛-inch layer of melted paraffin wax over each glass. Store in a cool, dry, dark place.

Yield: 10 to 12 jelly glasses, about 2½ quarts

Cook's Note: Best made with fresh, native peaches.

Who Were the Minute Men?

Who and what were the Militia, Minute Men and the Continental Army? The Minute Men were a small elite force picked from the ranks of the militia who were highly trained and who could be ready in a minute. They took a stand at Concord's North Bridge, and "the shot heard 'round the world" began a revolution that brought freedom to the colonies and release from the yoke of British domination.

The Minute Men's weak point was the lack of a central command and with each company loyal to their own community, no one individual was the leader. In the aftermath of Bunker Hill, General George Washington brought together the colonial militia and the Minute Men to form the Continental Army. History knows the results of this strategic decision made by the "Father of Our Country."

Blueberry Jam

4½ cups prepared fruit
2 tablespoons lemon juice
7 cups sugar
1 bottle fruit pectin

1. Prepare fruit by crushing one layer at a time. Put in large saucepan.
2. Add lemon juice and sugar. Mix well. Place over high heat and bring to full rolling boil. Boil hard for 1 minute, stirring constantly. Remove from heat and add pectin at once. Skim off foam with metal spoon. Stir and skim for 5 minutes to cool slightly. Ladle into glasses. Cover at once with ⅛-inch hot paraffin.

Yield: About 12 cups

America's Most Painted Building

Recognized around the world, a dark red shack on Bearskin Neck Wharf is considered America's most painted building. It got its name from illustrator and teacher Lester Hornby who spent his summers in Rockport. Many of his pupils chose the old dilapidated shed on the inner harbor to sketch. Its position on the harbor is a natural scenic picture with the rocks, ships and buildings of the neck surrounding it. One day when a student brought a sketch to Hornby for criticism, Hornby exclaimed, "What? Motif #1 again!" Destroyed by a tidal surge during a storm in 1978 (and again in 1992), the landmark was soon rebuilt by all those who love this venerable red shack.

Highland Hotel's Seafood Cocktail Sauce

The Highland Hotel in Springfield was a wonderful place to dine in either the dining room or grill room. Throughout my youth, my family ate many wonderful meals there; my father and I were the last diners served in the grill room on the final night the Hotel was open. Regretfully, as is so often the case with progress, the wonderful old building was torn down forty years ago and today remains a parking lot...so much for progress. Due to some foresight, the window of the grill room was saved and is now located at the Sheraton Hotel. The crest and slogan, "Every Meal A Pleasant Memory," brought back many delightful recollections of the restaurant.

1 cup mayonnaise
½ cup catsup
½ cup chili sauce
2 tablespoons horseradish, prepared
1 red or green pepper, chopped fine
½ teaspoon Worcestershire sauce
¼ teaspoon paprika
Pinch curry powder

1. Blend all ingredients. Mix well.
2. Keep refrigerated. Cocktail sauce will keep for several weeks.

Tomato Mayonnaise

2 egg yolks
½ teaspoon salt
1½ teaspoons strained, fresh lemon juice
¾ cup vegetable oil
½ cup olive oil
1 pound tomatoes, peeled, seeded and finely chopped

1. In a food processor with a plastic mixing blade, place the egg yolks, salt and lemon juice. Whirl on medium speed for about 2 minutes, until the mixture is pale yellow.
2. In a large measuring cup with a spout, combine the vegetable and olive oils. Through the feed tube, with the processor running continuously, add the oil drop by drop. Scrape down the sides of the bowl periodically. When half the oil has been added and the mixture has thickened, slowly add the remaining oil in a very thin stream.
3. After all the oil has been incorporated, add the chopped tomatoes with any juices that have accumulated, and whirl until the mayonnaise is well mixed.

Cook's Note:
The mayonnaise may also be made by hand, beating continuously while adding the oil. It is delicious on sandwiches in place of other condiments. Must be refrigerated.

Cranberry Vinaigrette

3 tablespoons red wine vinegar
⅓ cup olive oil
¼ cup fresh cranberries
1 tablespoon Dijon mustard
½ teaspoon minced garlic
½ teaspoon salt
½ teaspoon black pepper, freshly ground
2 tablespoons water

1. In a blender or food processor, combine all ingredients. Process until smooth.
2. Refrigerate. Vinaigrette will keep several days.

Sherry Vinaigrette

1 tablespoon shallots, minced
½ teaspoon Dijon mustard
Salt and pepper to taste
1 tablespoon sherry wine vinegar
3 tablespoons extra-virgin olive oil

1. Mix all ingredients together and let sit overnight in the refrigerator.
2. Terrific on salads with apples, toasted nuts, pears and/or blue cheese.

Cook's Note:
I had this vinaigrette on a salad that included pumpkin, infused with maple syrup and butter, and hazelnuts. It was absolutely delicious.

Balsamic Vinaigrette

½ cup extra virgin olive oil
½ cup balsamic vinegar
1 clove garlic, crushed and minced finely
1 teaspoon ground mustard
Pinch salt
Freshly ground pepper

1. In a small bowl, whisk together vinegar, garlic, mustard, salt and pepper.
2. Gradually add olive oil, whisking continuously.

Cook's Note:
Fresh herbs add a different taste depending on dish. For instance, add some finely chopped basil for salads with tomatoes or chopped tarragon on a salad with grilled chicken.

Maple Vinaigrette

½ teaspoon salt
¼ teaspoon pepper, freshly ground
2 tablespoons pure maple syrup
1 teaspoon Dijon mustard
2 tablespoons red wine vinegar
½ cup vegetable oil

Mix all ingredients together in a jar by hand. For a creamier dressing, use a hand blender.

Special New England Meals

Eastham

Can You Pronounce It?

Lake Chargoggaggoggmanchaugagoggchaubunagungamaug, better known as Webster Lake, is the fifth longest word in the world and the longest name for a lake. According to Wise Owl, chief of the Chaubungungamaugg band of Nipmuck, it is an Indian word for a neutral fishing place near a boundary (a meeting and fishing spot shared by several Indian tribes). A more popular definition of the Lake is, "You fish on your side, I fish on my side, nobody fish in the middle."

Red Flannel Hash

It has been said in our family that the reason I love the New England Boiled Dinner is for the hash the next day. This is my very favorite meal.

Leftover vegetables from New England Boiled Dinner
Beets
Cooked corned beef or smoked shoulder
1-2 tablespoons of butter (or vegetable oil spray)

1. Heat large fry pan on stove at medium high and put either butter or spray with vegetable oil to preheat sticking.
2. Cube potatoes, turnip, carrots beets and cabbage into quarter-inch pieces. Put in frying pan.
3. Cut leftover meat into cubes and place in pan. Mix until well blended and heated through. Serve at once.

New England Boiled Dinner

1 smoked shoulder or flat corned beef
8 potatoes, peeled
1 package small carrots
1 turnip or rutabaga
1 small head of cabbage

1. Put smoked shoulder or corned beef in large pot and cover with water. Slowly bring meat to boil and reduce heat and let meat simmer for 2 to 3 hours or until a sharp knife slides easily through the meat. When cooked remove from water and cover.

2. While meat is cooking, prepare vegetables and place them in cold water until ready to cook. Peel potatoes and cut in half; slice and peel turnip; cut cabbage into eights; and wash carrots.

3. About 40 minutes before serving, put turnip or rutabaga in broth from meat. Cook at medium-high heat for 10 to 15 minutes; add the potatoes, carrots and place cabbage on top. For the last 10 minutes, place meat on top of vegetables to warm. Continue cooking until potatoes and turnip are fork-tender.

4. Remove from heat. Slice meat and place on platter. Drain and separate vegetables. Put vegetable in bowls and serve.

Yield: 4 servings with enough for seconds and Red Flannel Hash.

Cook's Note:
This dinner is as old as New England. It is one of my favorites, and whenever I visit friends in other parts of the country, they inevitably ask me to prepare this meal for them. Serve with pickled beets (see Vegetables and Side Dishes chapter).

Clamming It Up

Oh for the taste of delicious clams, lobsters, potatoes, corn and oysters cooked in the earth and feasted upon as the waves break over the shore. It is believed that the Wampanoag Indians, who cooked their food in a hole in the ground, created the first clambake. The same method is used today, hundreds of years later, to create a marvelous meal. While eating clams steamed under mounds of seaweed is a terrific experience, in the 21st century whenever a meal consisting of clams, mussels, oysters, lobsters and corn on the cob are served, it is considered a "clambake." You can do it on a grill or in the middle of January in your kitchen.

New England Clambake

8 (1-pound) lobsters
8 pounds steamers
16 ears sweet corn
½ pound butter

1. In the bottom of a large pot (you will need three pots in all), place about an inch of water. Add steamers and cook for about 15 minutes until the shells open.
2. At the same time, fill a extra large pot ¾ full and bring to a boil. This should take about as long as it takes to cook the steamers. When at a rolling boil, drop lobsters in head first. Return to boil and reduce temperature.
3. In your third pot place the corn and bring to boil, then reduce heat and let corn cooked for about 15 to 20 minutes
4. Serve the steamers and enjoy with clam broth and melted butter while the lobsters cook (this will take about 20 minutes).
5. Check lobsters to make sure they are cooked, and serve hot with melted butter. At the same time, serve corn. This can get a bit messy so you might want to give your guests lots of napkins and perhaps a linen cloth tea towel or bib.

Yield: 8 servings

Authentic Clam Bake

This recipe is for those who want to have a clambake the way our forefathers cooked.

1. Start by digging a hole in the sand 2' wide x 4' long x 1½' deep. Line the hole with stones from the beach (most New England beaches have plenty of rocks and stones); then build a fire in the hole and surround the fire with more rocks. Let the fire burn for 2 to 3 hours, making sure it is well-fed with driftwood.
2. Remove hot embers from the hole and dispose of them safely, making sure they are extinguished. Arrange hot stones over bottom of the hole. Cover with about a half bushel of wet seaweed.
3. Quickly layer the food on top of the hot stones in the following order: clams, corn and lobsters. Cover with clean wet linen-type cloth. Add more seaweed.
4. Cover end hole with a tarpaulin sealing in the steam. Let some steam to escape to prevent a buildup of pressure. The bake should be completed within 45 minutes. If you have added items such as potatoes, plan on the bake taking longer.
5. Serve clams with melted butter. Put butter in a saucepan and cover tightly with foil and place on edge of the bake. Enjoy!

Cook's Note:
Some people like to add potatoes, onions, hot dogs, sausage and all sorts of good things, but for me the simplicity of the above recipe is delicious. A pound of steamers per person is just about right, but it is always good to have a few extra pounds of clams and another lobster or two handy in case you have a few big appetites. For dessert, serve ice cold watermelon.

Clam Cakes

1½ cups flour
1½ teaspoons baking powder
½ teaspoon salt
¼ teaspoon pepper
1 egg, beaten
2 (6.5-ounce) cans minced clams
Milk

1. Sift dry ingredients into egg.
2. Lightly stir in clams and juice. Add only enough milk to moisten.
3. Heat oil in frying oil until hot, but not smoking.
4. Drop batter by the tablespoon into hot oil. Cook a few minutes and then turn clams using a metal-slotted spoon. Drain on paper toweling.

Cook's Note: Do not make clams too large as the center will not cook and they will be doughy.

Codfish Aristocracy

Some countries have royalty, but only Massachusetts had the codfish aristocracy. These were families who earned their fortunes from fishing. There are a multitude of stories regarding the sacred cod. Cod was used to trade for spices, coffee and molasses from the West Indies, or in Europe for wine and other foods. For over 200 years at the State House on Beacon Hill, a four-foot carved cod has hung in the House of Representatives chambers, while a mackerel is worked into the design of the chandelier in the Senate chambers.

Cod Fish Cakes

1 box salt cod
4 medium potatoes, cubed
1 medium onion, diced
6 slices bacon, diced and cooked
1-2 tablespoons butter

1. Soak salt cod overnight, changing water frequently.
2. Dice bacon and cook over medium-high heat until crisp, stirring frequently.
3. Drain bacon, reserving 1 to 2 tablespoons. Place onion in pan and cook until soft and clear. Mash cooked potatoes.
4. Mix cod, bacon, potatoes and onion in a large bowl. With an ice cream scoop, make cod fish patties.
5. Melt butter in fry pan, place cakes in pan and cook until golden brown on both sides. Serve hot.

Yield: 4 to 6 servings

Oyster Stew

In old New England, a bowl of piping hot oyster stew formed the traditional Christmas Eve supper. In England, it was customary to serve oysters on Christmas. Therefore it was quite natural for them to continue the tradition since their new country had an abundance of delicately flavored oysters.

1 pint oysters (with liquid)
¼ cup butter
1 cup light cream, scalded
½ teaspoon paprika
3 cups milk, scalded
Freshly ground pepper
½ teaspoon salt

1. Pick over oysters. Put oysters with their liquid in the top of a double boiler. Make sure the water in the bottom half is boiling, but do not let the water touch the top pan.
2. Cook in butter and oyster liquid until edges curl.
3. Add cream, milk, salt and pepper. Heat to boiling and serve. Garnish with paprika or parsley.
4. Serve at once with crackers, preferably common crackers.

Yield: 4 servings

Mayflower Succotash

This is a dish that early settlers learned from their Indian neighbors, the Narragansetts. Its original name was "misickquatash," meaning the grains are whole.

1 cup fresh kernel corn
1 cup fresh cranberry bean, shelled
3 tablespoons butter
½ cup onion, chopped
½ cup cream
Salt and pepper to taste

1. In medium pot, cook fresh corn and beans in a little water for 30 minutes; drain. This will create juices known as bean liquor.
2. Melt butter in pan and sauté onions until translucent. Mix with beans and corn; add salt and pepper to taste.
3. Just before serving, add a little cream.

Yield: 4 servings

Sons of Liberty

The Sons of Liberty were a rather secretive group of shopkeepers and artisans. Initially, they were brought together to agitate against the Stamp Act. Within a short period of time, the group grew from the Loyal Nine to over 2,000 men. They harassed the Distributor of Stamps in Massachusetts and throughout the colonies with their objective being to force the distributors to resign. Their strongest weapon proved to be the newspaper and not mob violence. When the Stamp Act went into effect on November 1, 1765, it was ignored by the majority of colonists. Their motto, "No Taxation Without Representation," was one of the driving forces for the Revolutionary War.

Phoebe's Baked Beans

2 pounds navy pea beans
1 teaspoon baking soda
1 onion, peeled and quartered
½ pound salt pork, cubed
2 teaspoons dry mustard
½ teaspoon salt
Pinch black pepper
½ cup brown sugar
1 cup molasses

Cook's Note:
Rather than using a crockpot, try a beanpot and cook in the oven at the same temperature.

1. Soak beans overnight in cold water and drain.
2. Barely cover beans with cold water. Add baking soda and onion and bring to a boil; reduce heat and simmer for 15 minutes.
3. Set temperature of crockpot or oven to 275° and place beans and onion in pot. Place salt pork in center of beans with fat side down.
4. Add salt, pepper, brown sugar, mustard, molasses and enough water to cover by ¼-inch.
5. Cover and bake slowly for 6 to 8 hours, occasionally stirring. Add more water as needed.
6. Taste test beans, if not sweet enough, add more molasses or brown sugar to the beans.
7. For the last 30 minutes, remove cover and increase temperature to 350° and continue cooking. Serve with hot dogs or cod fish cakes.

Yield: 10 to 12 servings

"Old Greylock...You Are Ours"

In the northwest corner of Massachusetts in the towns of Lanesborough and Adams, there reigns the most beloved summit – Mount Greylock. At 3,491 feet, it doesn't begin to compete with the world's tallest mountains. Many poets, including Thoreau, have written tributes to the mountain. My favorite tribute comes from Tom Haines of the Boston Globe:

> *"This is what it is to be the tallest in a state long settled, a land long tilled and treed and left to grow again, a land where to be the best is to be embraced, owned. Oh yes, old Greylock, you are worshipped. Though you are not Everest, nor McKinley, nor even Mount Marcy, you are ours."*

Fiddleheads Ferns in Brown Butter

The fiddlehead is the soft, budding heat of the ostrich or fiddlehead fern. It is referred to as the fiddlehead because it resembles the scrolling head of a violin. Its flavor is a delicate cross between asparagus and spinach. Available for only a few weeks in the spring, they are highly prized by gourmet cooks.

½ teaspoon salt
4 tablespoons unsalted butter
½ pound fiddlehead ferns
Salt and pepper to taste

1. Fill a 2- or 3-quart saucepan with water to within two inches of rim; add salt. Bring water to a boil. Drop in fiddleheads, and cook over moderate heat until tender, about 5 minutes.
2. Drain immediately. Rinse under cold water to stop any further cooking and drain again.
3. Melt butter in a 12-inch skillet over moderately-high heat, shaking the pan vigorously until butter just starts to turn brown and smell nutty, about 2 minutes. Be careful not to let butter burn. Add fiddleheads; toss to coat and cook until reheated. Season with salt and pepper. Serve immediately.

Yield: 4 servings

Farmers Rebel

Settlers came to farm the fertile fields of the Connecticut River Valley and to benefit from the lucrative fur trade. Following the War of Independence, they hoped for peace under a new government that still eluded many Connecticut River residents, especially farmers.

The farmers returned home from the War to find high taxes and mortgage payments. Initially they sought relief through the courts, but when this failed, Shays' Rebellion began in August 1786. In late December, the farmers attacked the court in Springfield and when that failed, they assaulted the federal arsenal. As a result of Shays' Rebellion, the Constitutional Convention reconvened in Philadelphia where the weak Articles of Confederation were replaced by a strong constitution.

Cranberry, Apple, Sausage and Corn Bread Stuffing

1 pound bulk sausage meat
1 medium sweet onion, diced
1 large apple, Macoun or Cortland
Salt and pepper to taste
1½ cups cranberries, quartered
Corn bread
4 stalks celery, diced

1. Make corn bread recipe (see Breads and Brunch chapter). Let cool. Crumble in medium size casserole.
2. Brown sausage in skillet, pour off any fat and pat sausage dry.
3. Add onion, celery, apples and cranberries. Sauté until fruits and vegetables are soft.
4. Add sausage mixture to crumbled corn bread. If dry, add chicken broth until desired consistency is reach — moist, but not wet.
5. Refrigerate for a few hours to allow flavor to mingle, then bake at 350° for 40 to 45 minutes. Add more chicken broth if necessary, to prevent dressing from drying out.

A Necklace Like No Other

The Emerald Necklace is a park that begins at Back Bay Fens near Charlesgate East and continues for over six miles through Leverett Pond, then to Jamaica Pond and on to the Arnold Arboretum and Franklin Park.

Designed by Frederick Law Olmsted, designer of New York's Central Park, this remarkable public park system is enjoyed by thousands annually. Olmsted saw parks as the self-preserving instinct of civilization. He believed that nature was invaluable in restoring the human mind and spirit. Since the early 1990s, over $60 million has been spent to restore the parks to their previous beauty. In 1997, the Emerald Necklace Conservancy was formed to restore and preserve the Emerald Necklace for the future.

Oyster Dressing

1 pint oysters
½ cup celery, finely chopped
½ cup onion, chopped
4 tablespoons butter
4 cups small dry bread cubes
1 tablespoon parsley, chopped
1 teaspoon salt
⅛ teaspoon poultry seasoning
⅛ teaspoon pepper

1. Drain oysters, saving broth, and chop.
2. Sauté celery and onion in butter until tender.
3. Combine oysters, cooked vegetables, bread cubes and seasonings. Mix thoroughly. If mixture is dry, moisten with oyster broth.
4. Cook at 350º for 40 to 45 minutes, or until heated through.

Boston Tea Party

"Fellow countrymen, we cannot afford to give a single inch! If we retreat now, everything we have done becomes useless! If Hutchinson [Governor of Massachusetts] will not send tea back to England, perhaps we can brew a pot of it especially for him."

Samuel Adams
December 16, 1773

So began the famous or infamous Boston Tea Party. In opposition to a tea tax established by the British Parliament in the Tea Act of 1773, Samuel Adams and about 60 men disguised themselves as Mohawk Indians and boarded three ships at Griffin's Wharf – the Dartmouth, the Eleanor and the Beaver. The "Indians" and members of the crew tossed 342 chests of tea valued at 18,000 pounds into the Boston Harbor. In ensuing months, similar incidents occurred in New York, Maryland and New Jersey.

Boston Brown Bread

1½ cups raisins
1½ cups boiling water
1 cup brown sugar, firmly packed
4 teaspoons shortening
1 egg
1 teaspoon molasses
1 teaspoon salt
2 teaspoons baking soda
2⅔ cups all-purpose flour
½ cup chopped pecans

1. Preheat oven to 350°.
2. Combine raisins and water in a small bowl; set aside to cool.
3. Combine brown sugar, shortening, egg and molasses; beat well.
4. Stir in salt, soda, flour and raisin mixture. Stir in nuts.
5. Spoon into 4 greased (16-ounce) cans
6. Bake at 350° for 1 hour or until done. Cool slightly before removing from cans.

Yield: 4 loaves

What is Hasty Pudding?

In 1795, twenty-one Harvard students organized a new on-campus society whose purpose was "to cultivate the social affections and cherish the feelings of friendship and patriotism." Moreover, "each member in alphabetical order shall provide a pot of hasty pudding for every meeting." Hence, the Hasty Pudding Society was formed and the group has met every year since 1891, with the exception of during World Wars I and II.

Today, Hasty Pudding is a theatrical organization. None of this enlightening information answers the question, "What is hasty pudding?" It is a pudding made of flour or corn meal stirred in boiling milk or water to a consistency of a thick batter. It certainly doesn't sound very appetizing. The name comes from the fact that it could be quickly made. The recipe below is much tastier and a wonderful side dish.

Corn Pudding

2 cups white whole kernel corn
1 teaspoon salt
4 teaspoons sugar
4 ounces flour
2 ounces butter, melted
1 quart milk
4 eggs

1. Preheat oven to 450º.
2. In a casserole dish, mix corn, salt, flour, sugar and butter. Beat eggs and add to milk. Stir into the corn mixture.
3. Place in oven for 10 minutes. Remove and stir with long-prong fork, disturbing the top as little as possible. Repeat this step three times.
4. Return to oven for 10 to 15 minutes. Top should be lightly brown; pudding should be firm.

Yield: 6 to 8 servings

Durgin Park Saves Quincy Market

Generations of Bostonians and visitors are ever so grateful that John Durgin, Eldridge Park and John Chandler began a partnership over a century and a half ago creating a restaurant known as Durgin Park. Since that time, the eatery has known a few changes in chefs and the Quincy Market that we have today is a direct result of Durgin Park being where it is.

While the building housing the restaurant was built in the mid 1700s, Quincy Market came into being 270 years later. The area surrounding Fanueil Hall was to be revitalized by tearing everything down and beginning anew. Bostonians were outraged because this meant that Durgin Park would also be torn down. This is the restaurant where fisherman brought their catch to be cooked and many famous, and infamous, politicians dined. Thanks goes to all the Bostonians for saving this beloved restaurant with its delicious corn bread, baked beans, and my favorite, Indian pudding.

Durgin Park's Indian Pudding

1 cup yellow cornmeal
½ cup dark molasses
¼ cup sugar
¼ cup butter
¼ teaspoon baking soda
Pinch of salt
2 eggs, lightly beaten
6 cups whole milk
Vanilla ice cream

1. Preheat oven to 275°. Grease a 2½ quart baking dish with vegetable shortening.
2. Combine cornmeal, molasses, sugar, butter, baking soda and salt in a large saucepan. Add eggs and stir in 3 cups of milk.
3. Cook over medium heat, stirring constantly with a wooden spoon, until the mixture thickens, but does not come to a boil.
4. Remove from heat and whisk in the remaining 3 cups of milk.
5. Pour batter into the baking dish and bake in oven for 2 to 2½ hours. When done, the center of the pudding should be firm to the touch and a crust formed on top.
6. Serve warm with vanilla ice cream or whipped cream.

Vegetables and Side Dishes

Hancock

Wizard of the Waves

On January 18, 1903, Guglielmo Marconi sent the first transatlantic telegram from President Theodore Roosevelt to his Majesty King Edward VII. It is hard to imagine that this remote corner of Cape Cod was a hot communications center, but from this point in Wellfleet, there was a clear open path to Europe. Most thought it improbable; even Thomas Edison doubted that wireless communication could occur between the continents.

In 1900 to prove his doubters wrong, Marconi bought the land and established Marconi's Wireless Telegraph Company (which later merged with RCA). A few minutes after Marconi sent the first telegram by Morse code to the King of England, a reply came addressed to "The President, White House, Washington." His achievement won him a Nobel laureate and the title, Wizard of the Waves.

Lemon Cabbage

1½ teaspoons butter
1½ tablespoons olive oil
1 teaspoon caraway seeds
1 medium cabbage, coarsely chopped
1 teaspoon lemon rind, grated
2 tablespoons lemon juice
½ teaspoon salt
½ teaspoon pepper

1. Heat butter and oil in a large skillet over medium-high heat for 2 minutes.
2. Add caraway seeds; cook one minute, stirring often.
3. Add cabbage, stir-fry 3 to 4 minutes. Cover, reduce heat, and steam until cabbage is tender, about 2 to 3 minutes.
4. Add lemon rind, lemon juice and seasonings; toss gently.
5. Serve hot.

Yield: 6 servings

Garden Medley Casserole

3 onions, sliced
2 tablespoons olive oil
2 medium potatoes, peeled and sliced thin
2 medium zucchini, thickly sliced
1 small eggplant, thinly sliced
Salt and freshly ground pepper to taste
1 green pepper, cored, seeded, sliced
2 tablespoons melted butter
½ teaspoon basil
2 cloves garlic, minced
3 large tomatoes, peeled and sliced

1. In a large dutch oven, sauté two of the onions in olive oil until tender. Add potatoes and cook until lightly browned.
2. Add zucchini and eggplant in two layers. Season with salt and pepper. Make a layer of the remaining onion slices and green pepper and season with salt and pepper.
3. Drizzle butter over the top and sprinkle with basil and garlic. Top with tomatoes and season again. Cover, bring to boil and simmer gently about 25 minutes, or until the vegetables are tender.
4. Serve hot or cold, spooning down to the bottom to catch all layers.

Yield: 6 servings

Creamed Spinach

2 (10-ounce) packages frozen chopped spinach, cooked and drained
½ cup chopped onion
2 tablespoons butter
6 ounces cream cheese
½ teaspoon salt
¼ teaspoon pepper
⅓ cup milk

1. Place onion and butter in large fry pan. Sauté onion until translucent.
2. Add cream cheese, salt and pepper; stir until smooth.
3. Blend in milk. Add spinach and continue cooking until mixture is heated through, about 6 to 8 minutes.

Yield: 6 to 8 servings

Connecting Two Bays

For over 300 years, men dreamed of a canal connecting Cape Cod Bay and Buzzards Bay. As early as 1697, the Massachusetts legislature authorized a commission to study the idea. It then took over 200 years to actually begin work on the canal.

If the Canal had been built in the early 1800s, the cost would have been under $1 million. However, by waiting another 100 years, the costs rose to over $12 million. In order to get the canal dug, the Canal Company imported 500 Italian immigrants to do the job. Finally, after five long years of exhausting and arduous work, the Cape Cod Canal opened on July 29, 1914 to a great deal of fanfare.

In 1928, the U.S. government took control of the Canal and built the Sagamore, Bourne and trestle bridges. In 1935, the U.S. Army Corps of Engineers widened the Canal to 480 feet and deepened it to a minimum depth of 32 feet at low tide. Today the Canal carries over 20,000 vessels and 24 million tons of cargo annually and is considered the widest sea-level canal in the world. Weary travelers who traverse the bridges above only wish that they too had been built wider.

Cucumbers in Sour Cream

2 english cucumbers
Salt
1 cup sour cream
2 tablespoons lemon juice
Fresh ground pepper
1 teaspoon salt
Paprika
Parsley, chopped
Chives

1. Peel and slice cucumbers as thin as possible. Let stand 1 hour in salted ice water. Drain and press dry with hands.
2. Mix together sour cream, lemon juice, salt, pepper, paprika and chives. Add mixture to cucumbers.
3. Sprinkle with chopped parsley. Chill before serving.

Pearl Onion with Cranberries

1½ pounds pearl onions
2 tablespoons butter
¼ cup sugar
2 cups cranberries, fresh or frozen
⅓ cup chicken broth
Salt and pepper to taste

1. Preheat oven to 400º.
2. Peel onions and drop in boiling water for 2 to 3 minutes; drain. Place in cool water.
3. Trim ends of onions, removing outer papery layer and thin transparent layer. Score root end.
4. In a large skillet, cook onions in butter until lightly browned. Stir onions in skillet occasionally to prevent sticking.
5. Add sugar and toss to coat. Add cranberries and seasonings. Add chicken broth and scrape bottom of skillet. Place onion in a non-aluminum 11x7-inch baking pan.
6. Bake for about 30 minutes until onions are soft and glazed.

Yield: 8 servings

Green Beans with Warm Mustard Vinaigrette

2 pounds fresh green beans, trimmed
2 shallots, minced
2 tablespoons Dijon mustard
2 tablespoons balsamic vinegar
½ cup olive oil
Salt and pepper to taste
¼ cup fresh dill, chopped

1. Heat a pot of water to boiling. Add green beans and cook until crisp, about 2 to 4 minutes. Drain well.
2. Place shallots, mustard, vinegar, oil, salt and pepper in small saucepan. Heat, whisking continuously, until mixture is just hot to the touch.
3. Toss hot green beans with dressing to coat. Add dill and toss to combine. Serve immediately.

Hancock Shaker Village

In 1783, the Hancock Shaker Village began with a few faithful followers. It wasn't until the mid-1800s that the Village grew to be what it is today. The most striking building at the Village is the Round Stone Barn. Designed by Elder William Deming, the barn was built in 1825 for $10,000. The circumference of the building is 270 feet with walls 21 feet high and from 2½ to 3½ feet in thickness. The octagonal structure on the top of the barn was added fifty years later to provide better ventilation. No one knows why Elder Deming constructed the barn as he did, but it remains truly an architectural marvel.

Pickled Beets

Bunch red beets (usually 4-5 beets)
1 medium Vidalia onion, sliced
White or wine vinegar

1. Remove beet greens and wash to get rid of any dirt. Place in medium pot with a cup or two of water.
2. Cook on medium heat until tender. Let cool.
3. When cool, peel and slice. Place in jar along with sliced onion. Pour beet juice over beets. Add vinegar to taste.
4. Place in refrigerator and marinate overnight before serving.
5. Serve with New England Boiled Dinner.

Cook's Note:
I usually use a 50/50 split of beet juice and vinegar, but this might be too strong for some.

Sautéd Vegetables

4 carrots, diagonally cut in ⅛-inch pieces
Pinch salt
6 tablespoons unsalted butter
1 medium onion, chopped
1 garlic clove, minced
1 large shallot, minced
4 small zucchini, diagonally cut in ⅛-inch pieces
½ pound fresh shiitake mushrooms, sliced ¼-inch thick
1 red bell pepper, julienne
½ pound snow peas, string removed
1 teaspoon raspberry vinegar
Salt
Freshly ground pepper

1. Bring small pot of water to boil; add pinch of salt and carrots. Blanch carrots for about 5 minutes. Remove from heat; drain and immerse in cold water for a few minutes; drain.
2. Melt butter in large skillet. Add onions, clove and shallots and sauté for 2 to 3 minutes. Add blanched carrots and continue sautéing for another 5 minutes.
3. Add zucchini and mushrooms and continue sautéing for 5 more minutes. Finally, add the bell pepper, snow peas and raspberry vinegar; continue sautéing another 3 to 5 minutes.
4. Season with salt and pepper and serve immediately.

Yield: 6 servings

Gingered Carrots

7-8 carrots
1 tablespoon sugar
1 teaspoon cornstarch
¼ teaspoon salt
¼ teaspoon ground ginger
¼ cup orange juice
2 tablespoons butter
Chopped parsley

1. Cut carrots on the bias into ⅛- to ¼-inch thick slices. Cook, covered in boiling, salted water until just tender; about 7 to 10 minutes. Drain.
2. Combine sugar, cornstarch, salt and ginger in a small saucepan. Add orange juice and cook, stirring constantly, until mixture thickens and bubbles. Boil 1 minute then stir in butter. Pour over hot carrots and toss.
3. Garnish with chopped parsley.

Cook's Note:
Carrots can be prepared ahead of time and simply reheated before serving.

The Red Lion Inn

Built in 1773, the Stockbridge Inn, known today as The Red Lion Inn because of the red lion on its sign, began serving patrons and providing lodging. Over the next seven decades the Inn changed hands several times and it wasn't until the arrival of trains in the mid-1800s that the Inn became popular as the area became a destination for travelers from New York. In 1848, the then Stockbridge House was described in an article in the Pittsfield Sun, "[It] contains four pleasant and airy parlours, a spacious dining hall, and thirty-four large and well-ventilated rooms." It is one of the few remaining New England inns in continuous operation since the 18th century.

In 1896, the Stockbridge House caught fire and was totally destroyed. The Inn was rebuilt in eight months and was renamed The Red Lion Inn by its owners, the Treadways and Plumbs. Fortunately, the towns' people managed to save the Inn's collection of antique furniture, china, and accessories. Since 1968, the current owners, the Fitzpatrick family, have served the Inn well. They have brought the Inn into the 21st century with style and grace. Generations of visitors, famous, infamous, and not so famous, have sat on the porch and enjoyed a repose before heading to Tanglewood, the Norman Rockwell Museum, the theater or one of the other many attractions throughout the Berkshires.

Rissole Potatoes with Rosemary and Garlic

12 red bliss potatoes
6 tablespoons olive oil
6 tablespoons butter
2 tablespoons dried rosemary
2 tablespoons parsley, chopped
2 cloves garlic, cut in half
Salt and pepper to taste

1. Preheat oven to 375º.
2. Remove a ring of peel from around the circumference of each potato. Soak the potatoes in enough cold water to cover them to prevent discoloring until you are ready to use them.
3. Heat oil and butter in a sauté pan, add the rosemary and garlic, and sauté over low heat for 5 to 6 minutes, until the herbs have perfumed the oil, but have not browned.
4. Remove the herbs from the flavored oil and add the potatoes to the skillet. Sauté the potatoes over medium heat until golden, about 10 minutes.
5. Place the potatoes in a roasting pan, sprinkle them with salt and pepper.
6. Bake for 40 to 50 minutes or until tender. Sprinkle with chopped parsley just before serving.

Yield: 6 servings

Source: The Red Lion Inn Cookbook

Bounties of Fall

Fall brings many wonderful fruits and vegetables to the table that are not available at other times of the year. There is hubbard, acorn, golden acorn, pancake, spaghetti and butternut squash. They get the unusual names from either their shape or color. Spaghetti squash is so named because once it is cooked and cut in half, its insides resemble spaghetti.

Children of all ages enjoy a visit to area farms and fields to pick out that perfect pumpkin to carve for Halloween. While New Englanders love the colorful leaves of the fall, it reminds us that we must wait until next year to savor, once again, native produce and vegetables.

Apple and Butternut Squash

1 large butternut squash, peeled and cubed
2 large Granny Smith apples, cored and sliced
½ cup cranberries, halved
½ cup brown sugar
¼ cup butter, melted
1 tablespoon flour
1 teaspoon salt
½ teaspoon nutmeg

1. Preheat oven to 350º.
2. Place peeled and cubed squash into ungreased baking dish. Arrange apple slices on top; sprinkle with cranberries.
3. Combine remaining ingredients in a small bowl. Sprinkle mixture over squash and apples; cover with foil.
4. Bake 50 to 60 minutes, or until squash is tender.

Yield: 6 servings

Oven-Roasted Winter Squash

2 acorn squash
4 tablespoons butter
4 tablespoons honey or brown sugar
Sprinkle of cinnamon or nutmeg

1. Preheat oven to 350°.
2. Cut squash in half and scoop out the seeds. Add 1 tablespoon of butter and sugar or honey into each cavity. Sprinkle each with a dash of cinnamon or nutmeg.
3. Place squash in a roasting pan and add a little water to pan. Cover tightly with aluminum foil and bake for about 45 minutes.

Yield: 4 servings

Roasted Peppers and Snow Peas

2 (6-ounce) packages frozen snow peas
2 large sweet red peppers
2 tablespoons butter
1 clove garlic, minced
Salt and pepper to taste

1. Preheat oven to 450º.
2. Roast peppers in oven until blisters form; remove from oven and place in a brown paper bag and close. Let sit for 15 minutes to cool. Peel, seed and cut into strips.
3. Bring a large pot of salted water to boil; add pea pods, cover and turn off heat. Let sit for 2 minutes; drain and rinse immediately in cold water to stop cooking.
4. Melt butter in large sauté pan. Add garlic, pea pods, and pepper strips. Sauté just until vegetables are heated thorough. Season to taste; toss to mix.

Yield: 8 servings

The Adams Family

Only twice in American history has both a father and son been president of the United States. Long before the Bush family, there was the Adams family – John and John Quincy. John Adams served as vice president to George Washington for two terms and it was he who made the famous statement about the Office of Vice President. To his wife Abigail he said, "My country has in its wisdom contrived for me the most insignificant office that ever the invention of man contrived or his imagination."

His son, John Quincy, was the sixth president of the United States and served his country in many capacities, including secretary of state under President Monroe. After losing his bid for re-election, the citizens of Plymouth elected Quincy to the House of Representatives. He was known as "Old Man Eloquent" and fought for what he considered right until his death in 1848.

Asparagus with Orange Sauce

6 tablespoons butter or margarine
2 tablespoons freshly grated orange zest
¼ cup fresh orange juice
1½ pounds asparagus, trimmed

1. Combine butter (or margarine), orange zest and orange juice; bring to a boil. Reduce heat and simmer until mixture is reduced by half and slightly thickened.
2. At the same time, steam asparagus 5 to 7 minutes, or until tender.
3. To serve, pour orange sauce over asparagus.

Yield: 4 servings

Eggplant and Tomato Casserole

1 tablespoons butter, melted
1-2 medium eggplants, sliced ¼-inch thick
2 large tomatoes, sliced ¼-inch thick
1 tablespoon salt
1 teaspoon pepper
¼ cup scallion, minced
2 teaspoons oregano, finely chopped
3 tablespoons parsley, finely chopped
3 tablespoons basil, finely chopped
¼ cup dry breadcrumbs
½ cup lowfat Mozzarella cheese, shredded
¼ cup Parmesan cheese, grated

1. Preheat oven to 350º.
2. Place eggplant on a baking tray; do not overlap. Salt eggplant evenly and let stand for 10 to 15 minutes. Place on paper towel and allow to dry.
3. Spray a large baking dish with nonstick spray. Begin layering eggplant and tomatoes, alternating each vegetable (layer each halfway over the previous one).
4. Drizzle butter over top. In a medium bowl, combine herbs, breadcrumbs and cheeses; sprinkle over the top of casserole.
5. Bake uncovered for 20 to 30 minutes or until lightly browned.

Apricots and Carrots

1 medium onion, chopped
4 tablespoons butter
1 pound carrots, cut into thin julienne slices
¼ pound dried apricots, cut into strips
½ cup chicken broth or water
2 teaspoons wine vinegar
Salt and pepper to taste

1. Sauté onion in butter until transparent. Add carrots and apricots and stir-fry for 2 to 3 minutes. Add broth or water; cover and cook about 5 minutes. Uncover and cook until liquid is evaporated.
2. Stir in vinegar, salt and pepper. Serve hot.

Yield: 4 to 6 servings

A Cultural Factory

Is a factory a factory when it manufactures textiles or electronics, or when it houses one of the leading contemporary art museums? The answer is both. Mass MoCa opened in 1999 in a converted 27-building historic mill. More than a static display, the museum provides artists, cultural institutions and businesses with space, time and tools. The mediums are as varied as the artistic endeavor – sculpture, theater, dance, film, digital media and music. Creativity is at the core of the mission of Mass MoCa. Only a few years old, it already has an international reputation and is an artistic work in progress.

Zucchini Bradford

2 pounds small zucchini
½ chopped onion
1 stick butter
1 cup cheddar cheese, grated
½ cup Gruyère cheese, grated
1 cup sour cream
1 teaspoons salt
½ teaspoon paprika
¾ cup breadcrumbs
Parmesan cheese, freshly grated

1. Preheat oven to 350º.
2. Cook squash in boiling water until tender; drain.
3. Place in buttered, shallow 2½-quart baking dish.
4. Sauté onions in butter until tender. Add cheddar and Gruyère cheeses, sour cream, salt and paprika, stirring until cheeses melt. Pour over zucchini.
5. Sprinkle with breadcrumbs and Parmesan cheese.
6. Bake 30 to 45 minutes.

Yield: 8 servings

Summer Squash Casserole

5-6 small summer squash, sliced
1 medium onion, chopped
½ cup carrot, grated
1 cup sour cream
¼ cup milk
1 can cream of chicken soup
1 stick butter, melted
2¼ cups herb stuffing mix
½ cup cheddar cheese, grated

1. Preheat oven to 350º.
2. Sauté summer squash, onion and carrot until onion is translucent and squash is easily pierced with fork, but not soft; drain.
3. Mix with sour cream, milk and cream of chicken soup. Add dressing to melted butter and mix thoroughly.
4. In a 2-quart casserole, layer squash mixture with stuffing mix, starting with squash and ending with stuffing mix. Sprinkle top with cheddar cheese and remaining stuffing mix.
5. Bake for 30 minutes until top is golden and cheese melted.

Yield: 6 to 8 servings

Baked Sliced Eggplant

1 medium-sized eggplant
Salt
½ cup mayonnaise
1 scallion, finely minced
1 cup dry bread crumbs
½ cup grated Parmesan cheese

1. Preheat oven to 375°.
2. Peel eggplant and slice about ½-inch thick. Sprinkle with salt and let stand 20 minutes. Pat dry with paper toweling. Mix mayonnaise and scallions; spread on both sides of eggplant slices.
3. Combine breadcrumbs with cheese. Coat each side of eggplant slices with this mixture, place on a lightly oiled baking sheet.
4. Bake for 20 to 25 minutes, until golden and crisp.

Yield: 4 servings

The Angel of Hadley

Angels come in all forms, but on September 1, 1675 William Goffe saved the town of Hadley from an Indian raid. It seems Goffe appeared during a service at a Meeting House and organized the men inside, thereby preventing the raid. He left before the settlers could thank him. He became known as the "Angel of Hadley." It wasn't until 1760 that the Angel's identity became known. This same man was a member of a parliamentary tribunal that condemned King Charles I to death. When the King's son resumed the throne in 1660, he issued death warrants for Goffe and other members of the tribunal. The Reverend John Russell, of Hadley, hid Goffe and Edward Whalley (another member of the tribunal) for twelve years in his home.

Cranberry Squash

3 pounds butternut squash, peeled and cubed
2 tablespoons maple syrup
½ teaspoon salt
½ cup fresh or frozen cranberries
¼ cup sugar
2 tablespoons maple syrup

1. Preheat oven to 375°. Spray pan with cooking oil so squash does not stick.
2. In a shallow roasting pan, toss squash with 2 tablespoons maple syrup, and salt. Spread in single layer in shallow roasting pan and roast 35 to 40 minutes, turning frequently, until tender and golden. Drain squash before mixing with cranberry mixture.
3. In a small saucepan, combine cranberries, 2 tablespoons sugar and maple syrup. Cook over medium heat until sugar dissolves and coats cranberries. Toss cranberries and their syrup with squash.
4. Serve hot.

Yield: 6 servings

Apples, Turnip and Potatoes

2 pounds turnip, peeled, 1-inch squares
2 pounds potatoes, peeled, cut lengthwise
1½ pound apples, peeled, cored, cut 1-inch pieces
2 cups milk
10 tablespoons unsalted butter
Salt and pepper to taste

1. In large saucepan, cook turnip and potatoes in salted water until very tender, about 25 minutes. Drain, reserving ½ cup liquid.
2. Return turnip and potatoes to pot and mash.
3. Cover apples in heavy skillet in reserved liquid; cover and cook over low heat until apples are very tender, about 20 minutes. Mash apples. Mix apples with potatoes and turnip.
4. Bring milk to boil in heavy saucepan. Gradually beat milk and butter into apple/vegetable mixture. Stir over medium heat until butter melts and mixture is heated through. Season with salt and pepper.

Yield: 8 servings

Baked Sweet Potatoes with Apples

3 large sweet potatoes, peeled and sliced
4 large apples, peeled, cored, and sliced
½ cup maple syrup
¼ cup apple cider
3 tablespoons butter

1. Preheat oven to 375°.
2. In 13x9x2-inch glass baking dish, alternate potato and apple slices in rows, packing tightly.
3. Combine remaining ingredients in heavy medium saucepan and bring to boil over high heat. Pour hot syrup over potatoes and apples.
4. Cover dish with foil and bake for 1 hour. Uncover and reduce temperature to 350°. Bake until potatoes and apples are very tender and syrup is reduced to thick glaze, basting occasionally, about 45 minutes. Let stand 10 minutes before serving.

Yield: 8 servings

At the End of the Necklace

Named after Benjamin Franklin, Franklin Park in Roslindale and Roxbury is the largest single gem of the Emerald Necklace and home of the Franklin Park Zoo. Home to the nation's second-oldest municipal golf course, the Park offers many experiences to visitors. Whether walking, jogging, biking, picnicking or visiting the zoo, the Park's green meadows and hills are a sanctuary from city life. While at the Zoo, visit Little Joe, a 300-pound male "escape artist" gorilla. In late 2003, Little Joe escaped from the Zoo twice in two months. He is back on exhibit in a new home after a brief absence.

Maple-Orange Glazed Beets

2 pounds fresh beets
1 medium size sweet onion

Maple-Orange Sauce:
¼ cup maple syrup
2 tablespoons orange juice
1½ teaspoons Dijon mustard
½ teaspoon grated orange rind
Salt and pepper to taste

1. Preheat oven to 375°.
2. Scrub beets and trim roots; leave a portion of stem on each beet. Wrap beets and onion individually with aluminum foil; wrap tightly and place in a shallow baking dish.
3. Bake in oven for approximately 1 hour or until knife tender. Let cool; then, trim off stem and rub off skins. Cut beets into julienne strips. Peel onion and cut into ¼-inch slices. Cut each slice in half.
4. Combine maple syrup, orange juice, mustard, grated orange rind, salt and pepper in a large skillet. Bring to boil over medium heat, stirring frequently. Add beets and onion, and cook 2 minutes or until thoroughly heated, stirring constantly. Serve immediately.

Yield: 4 servings

Cheddar Potato Casserole

5 pounds red bliss potatoes
⅔ cup butter, melted
1 cup chopped onion
1 (12-ounce) can evaporated milk
4 eggs, beaten
2½ teaspoons salt
¼ teaspoon pepper
2¼ cups cheddar cheese, shredded

1. Peel potatoes and set aside in cold water to prevent discoloration.
2. Preheat oven to 350º. Grease or spray with nonstick spray a 9x13-inch baking dish.
3. Melt butter in a large skillet. Add onion and sauté until soft and translucent. Add evaporated milk; bring to a boil and then remove from heat.
4. In a large bowl, combine the eggs, salt, and pepper; beat until frothy. Shred to potatoes and add to the egg mixture; toss to combine.
5. Add milk mixture. Add 1½ cups of cheddar cheese to mixture and mix well.
6. Spoon into prepared casserole dish. Bake for 1 hour; remove from oven and top with remaining cheese. Bake for an additional 30 minutes. Cut into squares and serve hot.

Yield: 8 to 10 servings

Wild Rice with Apple

1½ cups water
½ cup orange juice
3 tablespoon lime juice
2 cups wild rice
2 cups long-grain rice
1 cup apple, peeled and chopped
1 cup frozen green peas, thawed

1. Combine water, orange and lime juice in a medium saucepan. Bring to boil; pour in long-grain and wild rice. Stir rice once, and only once; cover and reduce heat to simmer. Cook for 30 minutes, or until liquid is totally absorbed.
2. Mix cooked rice with apple and green peas. Serve hot with chicken or pork.

Yield: 6 servings

Women Helping Women

Over 125 years ago, Dr. Harriet Clisby, one of America's first women physicians, founded the Women's Union. It began as a service provider to women and an advocate for the many issues impacting the lives of women in the 1800s. Its role has changed little through the years.

In 1877, the Shop at the Union on Boylston Street opened for business. It sold crafts and foodstuffs made by women in order to assist them in supporting themselves and their families. The shop is a wonderful place to find unusual gifts, jewelry and speciality foods. Today, as then, most items are created by women artisans or by companies owned by women.

Lemon Rice with Almonds

2 teaspoons butter
6 tablespoons minced onion
1 cup long-grain rice
1 (14.5-ounce) can chicken broth
¼ cup fresh lemon juice
2 teaspoons lemon zest, freshly grated
¼ cup sliced almonds (optional)

1. Lightly toast almonds and chop coarsely.
2. In a saucepan, melt butter and sauté onion until clear, but not browned.
3. Stir in rice, coating well. Add enough water to chicken broth to equal 2 cups and add to rice mixture. Stir in lemon juice and zest.
4. Bring to a boil, reduce heat, cover and simmer for 20 minutes or until all liquid is absorbed. Remove from heat, stir in almonds, and serve.

Yield: 4 servings

Conversion for Metric System

Liquid Measures

1 gal	=	4 qt	=	8 pt	=	16 cups	=	128 fl oz	=	3.79L
½ gal	=	2 qt	=	4 pt	=	8 cups	=	64 fl oz	=	1.89L
¼ gal	=	1 qt	=	2 pt	=	4 cups	=	32 fl oz	=	.95L
		½ qt	=	1 pt	=	2 cups	=	16 fl oz	=	.47L
		¼ qt	=	½ pt	=	1 cup	=	8 fl oz	=	.24L

Dry Measures

1 cup	=	8 fl oz	=	16 tbsp	=	48 tsp	=	237ml
¾ cup	=	6 fl oz	=	12 tbsp	=	36 tsp	=	177ml
⅔ cup	=	5⅓ fl oz	=	10⅔ tbsp	=	32 tsp	=	158 ml
½ cup	=	4 fl oz	=	8 tbsp	=	24 tsp	=	118ml
⅓ cup	=	2⅔ fl oz	=	5⅓ tbsp	=	16 tsp	=	79ml
¼ cup	=	2 fl oz	=	4 tbsp	=	12 tsp	=	59ml
⅛ cup	=	1 fl oz	=	2 tbsp	=	6 tsp	=	30ml
				1 tbsp	=	3 tsp	=	15ml

Volume

(teaspoons x 5) = milliliters

(tablespoons x 15) = milliliters

(fluid ounces x 30) = milliliters

(cups x 0.24) = liters

(pints x 0.47) = liters

(quarts x 0.95) = liters

(gallons x 3.8) = liters

Weight

(ounces x 28) = grams

(pounds x 0.45) = kilograms

Fahrenheit to Celsius Temperature

Tc = (Tf-32) * (5/9)

To convert degrees Fahrenheit into degrees Celsius, first subtract 32 from the Fahrenheit temperature. Then multiply by 5 and divide by 9.

Herbs and Spices

Allspice: Sweet flavor. Good with fruits, desserts, breads, beef, pork, ham, yellow vegetables, tomato sauces and relishes.

Basil: Sweet flavor with a pungent tang and aromatic odor. Use whole or ground. Good with lamb, fish, roasts, stews, ground beef, tomato and tomato sauces, vegetables (particularly green beans), dressings and omelets.

Bay Leaves: Pungent flavor. Use whole leaf, but remove before serving. Good in vegetables dishes, seafood, stews and pickles.

Caraway: Spicy taste and aromatic smell. Use in cakes, breads, soups, cheese and sauerkraut.

Chives: Sweet, mild onion-like flavor. Excellent in salads, fish, poultry, cream soups and potatoes.

Cilantro: Aromatic, parsley-like flavor. Use fresh. Excellent in salads, fish, chicken, rice, beans and Mexican, Chinese and Italian dishes.

Cinnamon: Sweet flavor. Compatible with fruits, desserts, breads, tomato-meat sauces, yellow vegetables, beverages, pork, chicken and some beef dishes.

Cloves: Sweet, pungent flavor. Good with pickled fruits, desserts, baked goods, beverages, lamb, pork, corned beef, yellow vegetables, tomato sauces and beets.

Curry Powder: Spices are combined to proper proportions to give a distinct flavor to meat, poultry, fish and vegetables.

Dill: Both seeds and leaves are pungent and tangy. Leaves may be used as a garnish or cooked with fish, soup, dressings, potatoes and beans. Leaves or whole plant may be used to flavor pickles.

Fennel: Sweet, hot flavor. Both seeds and leaves are used. Use in small quantities in pies and baked goods. Leaves can be boiled with fish.

Ginger: A pungent root, this aromatic spice is solid fresh, dried or ground. Use in pickles, preserves, cakes, cookies, soups and meat dishes.

Marjoram: Aromatic with slightly bitter overtone. May be used both dried or green. Use to flavor fish, poultry, omelets, lamb, sausage, stews and stuffing.

Mint: Aromatic with a strong, cool flavor. Excellent in beverages, fish, lamb, sauces, soup and fruit desserts.

Oregano: Strong, aromatic odor with a pleasantly bitter undertone. Use whole or ground in Italian dishes, meats, fish, eggs, pizza, omelets, chili, stews, poultry and vegetables.

Paprika: A bright red pepper, this spice is used in meat, vegetables and soups or as a garnish for potatoes, salads or eggs.

Parsley: Best when used fresh, but can be used dried as a garnish or as a seasoning. Try in fish, omelets, soup, meat, stuffing and mixed greens.

Rosemary: Fresh, sweet and very aromatic. Can be used fresh or dried. Season fish, stuffing, beef, lamb, poultry, onions, eggs, bread and potatoes. Great in dressings.

Saffron: Orange-yellow in color, this spice flavors or colors foods. Use in soup, chicken, rice and breads.

Sage: Aromatic with slightly bitter taste. Use fresh or dried. The flowers are sometimes used in salads. May be used with fish, omelets, beef, poultry, stuffing and sausage.

Savory: Aromatic with slightly pungent taste. Use with vegetables, sauces, poultry and soups.

Tarragon: Leaves have a pungent, hot taste. Use to flavor sauces, salads, fish, poultry, tomatoes, eggs and dressings.

Thyme: Sprinkle leaves on fish or poultry before broiling or baking. Try with chowders, fish, meats, poultry, stews and tomatoes.

Tales Index

Recipe Index

Breakfast

Cakes

Cheese

Chicken (see Poultry)

Chocolate

Clams

Cookies

Side Dishes

Soup

Vegetables

To order additional copies of the Taste and Tales of Massachusetts

Write or send order form to:
Bass Pond Press
P.O. Box 6
East Longmeadow, MA 01028-0006
Telephone: 413-782-0924
Fax: 413-783-0926
Visit our website at www.basspondpress.com

Please include a check payable to Bass Pond Press. Cost is $19.95 plus $4.50 for shipping and handling. Massachusetts residents add 5% sales tax. For volume or wholesale orders, please call.

Name ____

Company ____

Address ____

City ______________________________ State ________ Zip ______________

Telephone ____________________________ Fax ____________________

Email ____

Look for the upcoming Taste and Tales of Florida!